The Basics of
STRENGTH TRAINING

Third Edition

John M. Cissik, CSCS

McGraw Hill **Custom Publishing**

Boston   Burr Ridge, IL   Dubuque, IA   Madison, WI   New York   San Francisco   St. Louis
Bangkok   Bogotá   Caracas   Lisbon   London   Madrid
Mexico City   Milan   New Delhi   Seoul   Singapore   Sydney   Taipei   Toronto

The Basics of **Strength Training**
Third Edition

2 3 4 5 6 7 8 9 0 QPD QPD 0 9 8 7

ISBN 0-07-353613-X

Editor: Barbara Duhon
Production Editor: Sue Culbertson
Cover Design: Maggie Lytle
Interior Design: Ronni Burnett
Printer/Binder: Quebecor World

TABLE OF CONTENTS

INTRODUCTION

This book has gone through some changes since the second edition. In an effort to make the book more readable, the references have been moved to the back of the book. Whenever a specific study is cited it will appear in the text, however those readers looking for more information should look at the back of the book.

The periodization and long-term programming design sections have been expanded and reworked. With the different authors, models, and approaches this can be an enormously confusing subject. As a result, the chapter on periodization discusses the most popular approaches and covers pro's and con's of each. The chapter on program design presents useful steps on how to incorporate this approach to training.

Where possible, the exercise technique chapters include the latest research on the safety and effects of the exercises in question. The field is slowly moving from superstition and myth and we are gradually getting a better understand of how various exercises impact the body.

The first chapter addresses background information. A basic understanding of physiology and biomechanics is helpful because programs and exercise techniques are based upon these concepts. The second chapter addresses the gains that one makes from strength training and points out that there is still a lot that we don't understand today. Chapter three covers safety issues; things like the importance of good technique, supervision, and equipment maintenance. The fourth chapter covers the components of a workout; everything from how and why we warm up for strength training, to the various classes of exercise included in strength and conditioning programs, to how and why to cool down. Chapter five reviews the principles of exercise as they apply to strength and conditioning programs. These are important to understand to ensure that programs are effective and safe. Chapters six and seven get into long-term program design issues. Chapter six reviews approaches to periodization of training and discusses their limitations. Chapter seven provides step-by-step information on how to use periodization of training. Chapter eight through fourteen get into techniques of specific exercises. How to do the exercises, progressions, safety, spotting, common errors, and variations are included for the exercises described.

Strength and conditioning is a field that changes every few years. Those things we thought we knew, those things that we took for granted, have a habit of evolving which requires us to rethink how we do things. Hopefully this edition reflects all of that.

ACKNOWLEDGEMENTS

There are a number of people who I would like to thank for their help in the preparation of this book. The models who appear in these pictures deserve a special thank you, not only for their time but for discovering that it is more difficult to hold those positions than most people realize. I'd like to thank Brandi Garcia for working so hard to look serious; Shigeaki Meguro, NSCA-CPT for his patience while waiting for the camera to recharge; Joe Randick, CSCS for his help, even though he didn't know what he was getting into, and Chuck Smith who *did* know what he was getting into.

I'd like to thank Texas Woman's University for the use of their facilities. I'd also like to thank Monica Mendez-Grant, PhD, for taking a chance on me a few years ago even though I've probably contributed to an increase in her stress since then.

I'd like thank Ernie Kirkham at Texas A&M University for his help, encouragement, friendship, and evil sense of humor over the years. Ernie, I'll finally be honest – as long as I'm writing this book there will not be group hug or venture dynamic chapters.

Finally, I'd like to thank my wife Ewa Cissik, DVM, for her patience and support.

SCIENCE OF STRENGTH TRAINING

Science is frequently a topic that makes individuals apprehensive. This should not be the case as it is an important area to have a handle on because it explains why things are done the way they are. The goal of this chapter is to present the reader with a basic idea of how things work and why. Obviously a large book could be written on these topics. This is not meant to be an exhaustive look at the science behind strength training; rather it is meant to present the essentials in a simple and straightforward manner.

This chapter will discus the types of muscles in the human body and how skeletal muscle is structured. Next, this chapter will provide an overview of how muscular contractions occur. It will cover the types of muscular contractions and what factors affect how much force the muscles can produce. It will touch on how the body fuels movement. Finally, it will cover some of the basic biomechanical principles behind strength training.

TYPES OF MUSCLES

There are three different types of muscles in the body:

1. cardiac muscle,
2. smooth muscle, and
3. skeletal muscle.

Cardiac muscle makes up the heart. It is striated (i.e. has alternating light and dark-colored bands) and contains protein myofilaments called actin and myosin. Unlike skeletal and smooth muscle, cardiac muscle is set up so that when one cardiac muscle fiber is stimulated and begins to contract, this stimulation rapidly passes to many cardiac muscle fibers so that they contract together.

Smooth muscle makes up the walls of the blood vessels and organs. It also contains actin and myosin, although smooth muscle is not striated. Smooth muscle is responsible for things like dilation of the pupils, the hair on your arms standing on end when you are cold, etc. In other words, smooth muscle contractions are not typically under voluntary control.

Skeletal muscle is under voluntary control and is responsible for movement of the body. Like cardiac muscle, it is striated and contains both actin and myosin. This is the kind of muscle fiber that is developed through strength training. It is classified into two broad types of fibers:

- *Fast twitch muscle fibers* are capable of generating large amounts of force but they fatigue rapidly. Activities that develop fast twitch fibers include lifting weights, jumping, sprinting, and throwing. These are also known as Type II fibers or white fibers.

- *Slow twitch muscle fibers* generate small amounts of force but are difficult to fatigue. Walking, jogging, swimming, and standing are examples of activities that develop the slow twitch muscle fibers. These are also known as Type I fibers or red fibers.

In reality there are more than just two types of muscle fibers, there is a continuum of types that range from pure slow to pure fast with fiber types in-between that have qualities of both in varying degrees (see Staron, 1997 for more information).

Everyone is born with a certain percentage of fast twitch muscle fibers and a certain percentage of slow twitch muscle fibers. This is one of the things that helps to determine one's potential for a given sport (for example, someone with 80% slow twitch fibers will have better potential as a distance runner than someone with 20%). The bad news is that it does not appear that one can increase the percentage of fast twitch fibers although one can certainly develop the fibers that he/she possesses.

Now that we've reviewed the types of muscle that are in the body, it is time to look at how skeletal muscle is put together. This is important because it gives us information on how the muscles function.

SKELETAL MUSCLE STRUCTURE

Tendons attach muscles to bones. Running continuous with the tendon is a layer of connective tissue that covers the body's muscles. Under that layer of tissue are bundles of muscle fibers, each covered by another layer of connective tissue. Each individual muscle fiber is surrounded by still another layer of connective tissue. Each of these layers of connective tissue runs continuously with the tendon, this means that when tension is developed in a muscle fiber it can also develop tension in the tendon.

Muscle fibers are the cells of the muscles and they may run the entire length of the muscle. Like the muscle itself, they are composed of smaller units. Muscle fibers are made up of *myofibrils*, which are in turn divided into *sarcomeres*. Sarcomeres are the functional units of the muscle cell and are the smallest part of the muscle that contracts. According to McArdle, Katch, and Katch (1996), a single muscle fiber may contain 8000 myofibrils, each of which consists of 4500 sarcomeres! Each sarcomere is composed of even smaller proteins called *myofilaments*. There are two types of myofilaments, *actin* and *myosin*.

Actin and myosin are proteins that are important for the contraction of muscle fibers. Actin is also known as the thin filaments, myosin is also known as the thick filaments.

There is also a neural component to the structure of the muscle. Movements are controlled by the nervous system. *Motor units* transmit the commands from the brain and spinal cord to the muscles. A motor unit consists of a motor nerve fiber that runs from the spinal cord to the muscle and all of the muscle fibers that it innervates. The size of a motor unit depends on the function of the muscles in the motor unit. For producing small, fine tasks (like writing or eye movement) there are fewer muscle fibers in each motor unit. For larger, gross movements like walking there will be many fibers in each motor unit.

It is important to have an idea of how the muscle is put together because this affects how movements occur. The next part of this chapter will cover how the muscle contracts. Muscle contractions are responsible for movement of the human body.

HOW CONTRACTIONS OCCUR

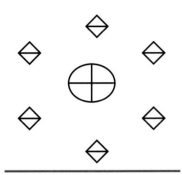

FIGURE 1-1 Arrangement of actin and myosin in space. The myosin is represented by the circle.

Myosin filaments are surrounded by actin filaments. Each myosin filament may be surrounded by six actin filaments (see figure 1-1).

Myosin contains globular heads that protrude away from the myosin filament. This is important to know because these heads will need to reach out and connect with the actin filaments in order for the muscles to contract.

Muscular contractions are governed by the *sliding filament theory of muscular contraction*. According to the sliding filament theory, for a contraction to occur the myosin's heads must connect to the actin filaments. This connection will slide the actin filaments inward along the myosin, causing the sarcomere to shorten. When enough sarcomeres shorten, the muscle fiber will shorten. When enough muscle fibers shorten, the muscle will shorten—moving the limb.

There are several types of muscular contractions. The next part of this chapter will discuss each of them.

TYPES OF MUSCULAR CONTRACTIONS

This section will review the three types of muscular contractions during strength training:

1. isometric,
2. isotonic, and
3. isokinetic.

Isometric Contractions

When a muscle contracts isometrically it does not change length. In other words, the force exerted by the muscle equals the resistance so the length of the muscle remains constant. An example of this is trying to push an immovable object like a wall. More common examples of isometric contractions occur when either there is too much weight on the bar, or too much fatigue, and the weight will not move. A great example of this can be seen when performing the bench press and hitting that sticking point just off the chest. If the bar won't budge then the lifter is performing an isometric contraction!

Isotonic Contractions

During isotonic contractions the muscle changes length. An isotonic contraction has two parts, *concentric contractions* and *eccentric contractions*.

Concentric contractions occur when the muscle shortens (i.e. the force applied is sufficient to overcome the resistance). An example of a concentric contraction would be holding a dumbbell and curling it towards the shoulder. As the dumbbell approaches the shoulder the biceps would be performing a concentric contraction.

Eccentric contractions occur when the muscle lengthen s (i.e. the force applied is less than the resistance so that the muscle lengthens). Taking the dumbbell curl example, lowering the dumbbell from the shoulder to the side would be an example of an eccentric contraction. Many researchers feel that it is eccentric contractions that cause muscle soreness after training sessions.

Isokinetic Contractions

During an isokinetic contraction, a maximal amount of force is exerted through the entire range of motion. This is important because, as we will discuss in the next section, muscles are not uniformly strong throughout their entire range of motion. In an isokinetic contraction the speed of movement is controlled so that when a certain speed is reached or exceeded, the resistance is increased. Examples of isokinetic devices are things like hydraulic machines, air cylinder shock absorber machines, or braking systems. True isokinetic machines are rarely seen in fitness centers and weight rooms, they tend to reside in rehabilitation centers and laboratories.

Now that you have an idea of what your muscles are capable of, it is time to look at what influences their ability to generate force.

FACTORS THAT AFFECT FORCE PRODUCTION

Many factors can influence how much force is produced in a muscle. The six that this book will discuss are:

1. physiological factors,
2. cross-sectional area,

3. angle of pennation,
4. velocity of shortening,
5. prestretching, and
6. length.

Physiological Factors

Force production is controlled in one of two ways: by the frequency of stimulation of motor units (also known as *rate coding*) and by the number of motor units activated. Both of these can be increased through training. Clearly, the more motor units one can recruit to lift an object, the more force he or she can exert. The faster motor units can be recruited, the faster force can be developed. Strength increases noticeably over the first several weeks of a strength training program, these strength gains are despite the fact that the muscles have not yet changed size. Much of that strength gain is thought to be due to these neural factors.

Cross-sectional Area

Simply put, bigger muscles are believed to be stronger muscles. This is because those muscles that have a larger cross-sectional area will have more sarcomeres in parallel, allowing more connections to be made between actin and myosin which will result in greater potential to produce force.

Angle of Pennation

Angle of pennation refers to the orientation of the muscle fibers with the tendon. Not all muscle fibers run straight up and down, some run at an angle. Those muscle fibers with a greater angle of pennation are able to generate more force because more sarcomeres are in parallel. However, those muscle fibers with less angle of pennation (i.e. fibers are straight up and down) are able to shorten more quickly (see Kumagi, et al 2000 for more information).

Velocity of Shortening

There is an inverse relationship between the amount of force a muscle can produce and the speed with which it contracts. In other words, during fast movements less force production is possible. This is thought to be due to the fact that when a fast movement occurs, there is less time for connections between actin and myosin to develop.

Prestretching

Prestretching a muscle prior to a contraction can enhance force production. This effect is due to two things, elastic energy and the stretch reflex. *Elastic energy* is thought to be built up and stored when a muscle is stretched quickly. When a muscle is stretched, it automatically tries to shorten (this is the *stretch reflex*). When the two items are combined (fast stretch, combined with extra energy, combined with the muscle trying to shorten on its own) this can result in more force production by the muscle. Prestretching forms the backbone of plyometric training, sprinting technique, and the Olympic-style lifts.

Length

The length of the muscle has an impact on its ability to exert force. Each muscle has an optimal length in terms of force generation; this is the point at which the greatest number of actin and myosin myofilaments are able to connect with one another. If the muscle is too long, then actin and myosin are too far apart making force production difficult. If the muscle is too short, then actin and myosin overlap making connections difficult. The barbell curl is a great example of putting this concept into effect. When one begins the curl, the biceps is lengthened which means that the actin and myosin are far apart—which is why the curl is difficult at the beginning of the exercise. As the elbow flexes and the barbell is curled up, the biceps shortens gradually making the exercise easier to perform. After a certain point (towards the last half of the exercise) the biceps is shortened, actin and myosin overlap, and the exercise goes back to being difficult again.

Another thing that can influence not only your ability to produce force, but also your ability to sustain exercise, is how much fuel is available. The last part of this chapter will discuss how your body fuels exercise.

BASIC BIOENERGETICS

At the most basic level, the energy that fuels movement comes from a compound called adenosine triphosphate or *ATP*. ATP consists of an adenosine group and three phosphates. When one of those phosphates is broken off, it releases energy, which is used for movement. ATP is also important because it fuels everything that takes place in the body, from movement to cellular reactions.

There are three pathways, or "energy systems" that are used to generate ATP:

1. the phosphagen system,
2. the lactic acid system, and
3. the oxidative (or aerobic) system.

The Phosphagen System

The phosphagen system provides ATP for short-term, high-intensity activities. When exercise first begins, this energy system is activated and begins to break down ATP that is stored in the muscles to fuel exercise. This energy system can fuel around six to ten seconds of exercise, i.e. one to three repetitions of an exercise, a vertical jump, running the 40, etc. This energy system is limited because only finite amounts of ATP are stored in the muscles. Fatigue can be staved off somewhat by resynthesizing ATP using a compound called creatine phosphate, but there are also finite amounts of creatine phosphate available. Ultimately, to exercise for longer than six to ten seconds, another way must be found to generate ATP to fuel the exercise.

The Lactic Acid System

This system breaks down carbohydrates in the form of glycogen (stored in the muscles and liver) or glucose (found in the blood) to produce ATP. This energy system can provide fuel for two to three minutes of exercise. It fuels high-intensity activities like sprints, running up hills, performing the two-minute sit-up test, etc.

The drawback to this energy system is that it produces a waste product, called lactic acid. Lactic acid interferes with the production of energy. Eventually lactic acid will shut down an exercise session. In order to exercise for longer than two to three minutes, one must reduce the intensity of the exercise in order to move into the next energy system.

The Oxidative (or Aerobic) System

The oxidative system uses oxygen to break down carbohydrates, fats, and sometimes protein to produce ATP. This system takes a long time to warm up, approximately two to three minutes. This system can only fuel relatively low-intensity aerobic exercise (jogging, walking, etc.). When the intensity of the exercise is increased, there will not be enough oxygen available; causing one to drop back into the lactic acid system. If the exercise remains at a steady, low-intensity then this system can fuel exercise almost indefinitely.

The thing to remember about the three energy systems is that they are used together. Whenever one starts exercising all three systems warm up. The system which will primarily fuel the exercise will depend upon how intense the exercise is and on how long the exercise will last.

Possessing a grasp of how the muscle functions and why is important because exercise and exercise programs are built upon this knowledge. This information will also allow one to be a more informed consumer when it comes to exercise programs, supplements, articles, etc. Failure to understand some of the science behind strength training and conditioning will lead to one being easy prey for scams that sound good.

As one can imagine, physics also has an impact on one's ability to lift weights, jump high, and run fast. It is important to understand several fundamental terms and principles in order to understand why exercises are performed with the techniques that they are.

The remainder of this chapter will cover basic kinematic terms, Newton's laws of motion, and levers and mechanical advantage.

KINEMATICS

Kinematics ignore the causes of motion (i.e. force) and describe an object's position in time and space.

The spatial element of kinematics refers to an object's position (i.e. where it is located). Changes in position is *displacement*. Displacement may occur in a perfectly straight line, known as *translation*. Translation is measured by meters and during translation all the parts of an object move the same distance, in the same direction, at the same time. To picture this, place a pen on the ground. Move it in a straight line. Notice that both ends of the pen moved the exact same distance. Displacement may also occur as a turning motion around an axis, called *rotation*. During rotation, different parts of an object may move different distances. To picture this concept, swing your arm in a big circle. Did your hand and your elbow move the same distance when making the circle? Rotation is measured by radians, each of which equals 57.3 degrees.

  Velocity refers to the rate of change in position with respect to time. Velocity is seldom constant, *acceleration* refers to the rate of change in velocity. It can be positive (i.e. velocity increases as one sprints from the starting blocks) or it can be negative (i.e. *deceleration*, one must slow down to change directions suddenly).

  While it is important to understand where objects are in space in time, strength and conditioning is about movement and force is necessary to move. Newton's laws of motion help one to understand how force controls movement.

NEWTON'S LAWS OF MOTION

Kinetics includes the consideration of force as the cause of motion. Newton's laws of motion help to explain how force causes motion and are very important to understand for strength and conditioning. Newton's laws of motion are:

- Law of Inertia: states that a force must start, stop, or alter motion. In other words, if a force does not act on an object it will continue to be at rest, or will continue in motion, indefinitely. *Inertia* refers to an object's resistance to a change in its motion. It is proportionate to the amount of matter in it, the more mass it has the more inertia it has. Not only is the amount of mass important, but in some cases such as rotary inertia (resistance to rotational movement) where the mass is located is also important. With rotary inertia, if the mass is further from the axis then there is more resistance to movement. This is why sprinters are told to bring their heels to their hips prior to cycling their legs forward in the sprinting motion.

- Law of Acceleration: states that the rate of change of momentum (how much motion an object has) is proportional to the applied force and takes place in the direction in which the force acts. This is where the equation force equals mass times acceleration comes in.

■ Law of Action/Reaction: states that for every action there is an equal and opposite reaction. For example, swinging the bar away from the body during the power clean frequently means that an athlete will be pushed backwards when receiving the bar – sometimes causing the athlete to fall over backwards!

Now that we've covered some of the laws governing kinetics, the last part of this chapter will cover the application of force and relate it back to what is occurring during strength training.

LEVERS AND MECHANICAL ADVANTAGE

The human body exerts force through a lever system. A lever is a rigid or semi-rigid body that, when subjected to a force whose line of action does not pass through it's pivot point, exerts force on any object impeding its ability to rotate. Figure 1-2 shows an example of a lever. The pivot point is referred to as the *fulcrum*. A *moment arm* refers to the shortest distance from the force vector (either applied force or resistive force) to the fulcrum. *Mechanical advantage* refers to the ratio of the moment arm through which the force is applied to the moment arm through with the resistive force act. If the moment arm of the applied force is larger, then there is a mechanical advantage.

There are three types of levers and each can be seen during strength training:

■ *First Class Lever:* where the muscle (or applied) force and the resistive force act on opposite sides of the fulcrum. The muscle force arm is shorter than the resistive force arm, so there is no mechanical advantage. Triceps pushdowns are a great example of these.

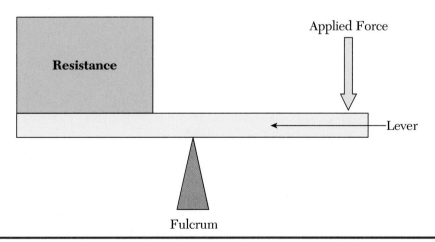

FIGURE 1-2 Sample level.

■ *Second Class Lever:* where the muscle force and the resistive force act on the same side of the fulcrum. The muscle force arm is longer than the resistive force arm, so there is a mechanical advantage. Standing calf raises are a great example of these.

■ *Third Class Lever:* where the muscle force and the resistive force act on the same side of the fulcrum. The muscle force arm is shorter than the resistive force arm, so there is no mechanical advantage. Barbell curls are a great example of these.

The science behind strength training is important to understand because it lays the foundation for why exercises are performed the way they are and why strength and conditioning programs are organized the way they are. Understanding the science allows one to take advantage of it through more effective exercise techniques and through strength and conditioning programs that can be designed to achieve specific goals.

BENEFITS OF STRENGTH TRAINING

Having discussed how things work, it is important to understand how the human body adapts to exercise. This is important because these adaptations are why we all exercise. Strength training has many benefits to the human body. This chapter will discuss several of the major ones; changes in muscle size and shape, changes in strength, changes in bone, and changes in one's ability to use and store energy.

Perhaps the first and most obvious benefit of strength training is that if one lifts weights, their muscles can become larger.

CHANGES IN MUSCLE SIZE AND SHAPE

When lifting weights, muscles may adapt by becoming larger. The growth of the muscles as a result of strength training is considered to be through *hypertrophy.* Hypertrophy refers to the increase in the cross-sectional area of existing muscle fibers; it does not refer to the laying down of new muscle fibers. Hypertrophy occurs from an increase in the thickness and the number of myofibrils. It is thought to be the primary mechanism that governs muscle growth.

Another approach to increasing the size of the muscles is through *hyperplasia.* Hyperplasia refers to increasing the number of existing muscle fibers. With hyperplasia, each muscle fiber splits into more fibers. Hyperplasia has not been seen in humans, though it has been found in cats. As a result it probably does not contribute significantly to an increase in skeletal muscle size as a result of strength training. The opposite of hypertrophy, the shrinking of muscles from disuse, is called *atrophy.*

McCall, et al (1996) investigated hypertrophy versus hyperplasia. They had fifteen college-age men lift weights for twelve weeks. Individuals worked out three times per week on eight exercises, performing three sets of ten repetitions with a minute rest in between each set. Weights were the participants' ten-repetition maximum (i.e. 10-RM). After twelve weeks, preacher curl strength increased by almost eight kilograms. Biceps brachii cross-sectional area increased by almost 13%! Triceps brachii cross-sectional area increased by approximately 25%! They found that both slow-twitch and fast-twitch fibers increased in size, though fast-twitch fibers increased more than slow-twitch. After twelve weeks of training, fiber type percentage (i.e. percent of slow versus fast) did not change and the number of muscle fibers remained the same. In other words, while participants got stronger and developed larger muscles they did not increase their percentage of fast-twitch fibers and they did not demonstrate hyperplasia.

Since hypertrophy is believed to be the primary mechanism governing muscle growth, it is going to dominate our discussion of how the muscles adapt to exercise in this chapter. The next section will discuss how hypertrophy occurs.

How Hypertrophy Occurs

How does hypertrophy occur? This is not very well understood even today (see Fluck, 2000 for a review). One of the most popular misunderstandings about hypertrophy is that it is from scar tissue. This idea states that when one lifts weights, one is actually breaking down the muscles. During the recovery period the muscles form scar tissues and this is what causes the muscles to grow. It appears today that exercise activates protein synthesis which causes the muscles to grow from training, not protein catabolism (i.e. not the breaking down of muscle cells). However, there may be some truth in the old view in that some experts believe that delayed onset muscle soreness may be caused by microtrauma experienced by the muscles following training.

Skeletal muscle fibers have a great capacity for change. This is referred to as *myoplasticity.* Myoplasticity is the potential to alter the gene expression in skeletal muscles. Altering the gene expression can lead to an increase or decrease in the amount of muscle proteins.

How does hypertrophy work? What exactly is going on in the muscles? Strength training increases the tension in the working muscles. This increases amino acid transport into the muscle cells, which enhances the synthesis of actin and myosin. The increase in protein synthesis may be seen by an increase in the number and the diameter of myofibrils. This is achieved by adding new myofilaments to the external layer of the myofibril, causing the diameter to increase. So, the act of lifting weights causes more amino acids to be transported to the outside layers of the myofibrils, which causes their diameter to increase. This causes the muscles to become larger.

The next question is: how does the muscle know to stimulate protein synthesis? How does protein synthesis form those new myofilaments? After all, you cannot make something from nothing! This is still not completely understood (see Fluck 2000 for a review). One possibility lies in the existence of satellite cells. These are dormant cells that lie under the basement membrane of the myofilaments. Upon stimulation, they "turn on," re-enter the cell cycle, and then differentiate to form myofibers by fusing with existing fibers or with themselves. Yan (2000) cites studies demonstrating that when satellite cells are destroyed by radiation, hypertrophy is not possible.

According to Brooks, Fahey, and White (1996), a number of factors influence a muscle's ability to undergo hypertrophy:

- Energy intake: inadequate levels will insure that the muscle cannot increase in size from training.
- Recruitment: if enough muscle fibers are not recruited (i.e. if the effort is not strenuous enough), then hypertrophy will not occur.
- Load: if the load is not heavy enough to warrant an adaptation, then hypertrophy will not occur.

As we have related, strength training can increase the size of existing muscle fibers. This is achieved by increasing the number of myofibrils and their diameter. For this to take place, the strength trainee must maintain an adequate energy intake and must insure that the exercise sessions are difficult enough to require the body to adapt.

Changes in the cross-sectional area are not the only adaptations to the muscle from training, the muscle's shape can also be changed.

Changes in Muscle Shape

As was seen in chapter one, muscle fibers run at an angle to the tendon, this is called the angle of pennation. This angle of pennation is not a static thing and can be influenced by training.

Kawakami, et al (1995) studied five men and had them perform triceps pushdowns with the right arm only for sixteen weeks. Subjects trained at five sets of eight repetitions at 80% of their maximum. After sixteen weeks the cross-sectional area of the triceps increased by almost 35%. However, the angle of pennation also increased by almost 30%. Kawakami, et al (2000) followed this study up by comparing body-builders with untrained individuals and found a strong relationship between muscle size and angle of pennation.

This has profound implications for training. Increasing the angle of pennation will increase the muscle's capacity to generate force. However, it will also decrease the muscle's velocity of shortening which could be important for certain athletic events. This is one of the reasons why certain sports should not be overloaded with bodybuilding training (see Cissik 2003 for an example).

Changes in muscle size and shape are not the only benefits to lifting weights. One can also develop stronger muscles as a result of training and, as we shall see, muscle size and shape can be important components to increasing muscular strength.

CHANGES IN MUSCULAR STRENGTH

Strength is the maximal amount of force one can exert, i.e. it is how much one can lift one time. *Explosive strength* is the ability to apply a maximum force in a minimal time. Explosive strength combines speed and strength.

Hypertrophy is usually more important to fitness buffs and recreational trainees, but strength and explosive strength are more important for athletes. This section is going to discuss what strength and explosive strength are and what factors contribute to their development.

Muscular Strength

Kurz (1991) and Zatsiorsky (1995) distinguish between two types of muscular strength:

1. *absolute muscular strength,* and
2. *relative muscular strength.*

Absolute muscular strength refers to the strength one can develop in a movement regardless of body weight. In other words, it could refer to the total weight lifted. Relative muscular strength is absolute strength divided by bodyweight. What is interesting about the two terms is that heavier athletes have a greater absolute muscular strength, but a lower relative muscular strength than their lighter counterparts. For example, if I bench press 300 pounds and you bench press 200 pounds, then I have a greater absolute muscular strength than you do. However, if I weigh 305 pounds, and you weigh 150 pounds, then I am only bench pressing 98% of my bodyweight while you are lifting 133% of yours. In this example you would have the greater relative strength.

Developing larger muscles will increase one's strength. However, larger muscles are not necessary for an increase in strength. One could increase his or her strength by training the central nervous system. Listed below are the factors that contribute to increasing one's muscular strength:

- muscle cross-sectional area,
- *intramuscular coordination,* and
- *intermuscular coordination.*

Muscles with a larger cross-sectional area are potentially going to be able to produce more force than muscles with a smaller cross-sectional area. The force production by a muscle is going to be limited by the number of actin/myosin filaments and the number of myofibrils in parallel. Muscles with a greater cross-sectional area will have more myofibrils per muscle fiber, a greater number of actin/myosin filaments, and a greater filament area density. In other words, muscles with a greater cross-sectional area will have more of the elements that are needed to produce force. Having said that, realize that muscle size is not necessary for increasing strength, although it helps after a certain point in training.

Intramuscular coordination refers to how many motor units are recruited during the effort, how quickly they fire, and whether the antagonistic motor units interfere with the movements. Training to increase muscular strength will result in more motor units being recruited during efforts, in increased speed with which they are recruited, and an increased inhibition of antagonistic motor units. If one can recruit more motor units, then more muscle fibers can be used during an exercise, which means more weight can be lifted. Increasing the speed of recruitment means the weights can be lifted more quickly, it also means one can make faster adjustments for the unexpected. Less inhibition means that the antagonistic muscles will provide less interference with the activity. All of this will combine to increase strength.

Intermuscular coordination refers to the skill part of performing strength training exercises. As one practices the exercises, one will learn how to perform them more optimally so that less energy is wasted in the execution of the exercises.

Strength is an important benefit of lifting weights. However, strength tends to be expressed slowly. This is often counter-productive to athletes who must be able to move quickly. For athletes, explosive strength is an important component to be developed through strength training.

Explosive Strength

As mentioned above, this is the ability to generate force quickly. This is an important attribute for athletics. Jumping, running, throwing, changing directions, hitting, serving, and kicking are just a few examples of athletic skills that require explosive strength.

The same factors that contributed to muscular strength also contribute to explosive strength; muscle cross-sectional area, intramuscular coordination, and intermuscular coordination.

Since strength is an important component of explosive strength, it is necessary to improve those qualities that improve strength. By increasing the cross-sectional area of the muscle, one increases the strength of the muscle. By increasing the strength of the muscle one potentially increases the explosive strength of the muscle. However, one must be careful that he or she does not increase strength at the expense of speed.

Just like with developing muscular strength, it is not necessary to increase the size of the muscles to increase explosive strength. In fact, in some sports this may be counter-productive because increasing body mass may make the sporting event more difficult (see Cissik 2003).

It is important to increase the number of motor units that are recruited during efforts. However, with explosive strength one also needs to focus on the rate at which motor units fire (i.e. rate coding). With explosive strength, the nervous system is an important component to develop. The nervous system controls how many motor units are recruited and how quickly they fire. Speed and explosive exercises are needed to cause the nervous system to adapt because one wants to be able to express strength *quickly*.

Training for strength alone will not necessarily increase explosive strength, one needs to perform exercises that emphasize expressing strength quickly (i.e. sprints, plyometrics, Olympic-style lifts, etc.). Garhammer (1993) reports that elite male weightlifters performing the snatch, clean, or jerk will generate approximately 34 watts of power per kilogram of bodyweight. By comparison, elite male powerlifters will generate approximately 12 watts of power per kilogram of bodyweight during the squat and deadlift and only four watts of power per kilogram of bodyweight during the bench press. In other words, while the bench press, squat, and deadlift are fine conditioning exercises they should not be relied upon for developing explosive strength.

The remainder of this chapter will discuss other adaptations from strength training such as those involving bone and the capacity to use and store energy.

CHANGES IN BONE

Exercise can have a positive affect on bone mineral density (BMD). Lack of exercise, especially with advancing age, can have a detrimental affect on BMD. Bone adapts to activity, or inactivity, according to Wolff's law. Wolff's law states that bone adapts to mechanical stress or loading by increasing mineralization in a particular region of the bone to increase the strength of the bone to withstand the stress.

Several authors have demonstrated that regular exercise can retard or inhibit the bone loss associated with old age and osteoporosis. However, most of those authors have demonstrated this using aerobic exercise. A number of studies have demonstrated the affects of various types of exercise on BMD. For example, Sabo, et al. (1996) have demonstrated that elite weightlifters and boxers have a greater BMD than controls and cyclists. Conroy, et al. (1993) showed that elite junior weightlifters have a greater BMD than age-matched controls. Colbert, et al. (1999) found that volleyball players have a greater BMD than age-matched controls.

While weight-bearing aerobic exercise and various types of sports participation have been established as having a positive affect on BMD, there have been fewer conclusive studies on strength training and BMD. Conroy, et al. (1993) found that elite junior weightlifters had a greater BMD at the spine, femoral neck, trochanter, and Ward's triangle than age-matched controls. Sabo, et al. (1996) found that elite weightlifters (world- and Olympic-champions) had a 23-30% increased BMD at the lumbar spine when compared with controls. The results of these studies make sense considering the nature of the sport of weightlifting. This sport requires the athlete to lift heavy objects from the floor over their head. Thus the lifter's entire body must support weights that are in excess of his or her own bodyweight.

The limitation of those studies is that most individuals do not participate in the sport of weightlifting and are not elite weightlifters. Rhodes, et al. (2000) studied women aged 65-75 and had them participate in regular weight training sessions for twelve months. The women performed exercises such as the bench press, leg press, arm curl, etc. on a Universal gym. After one year of training their strength improved by 20-50% when compared with the control group. However, the increases in BMD, while existing, was statistically insignificant. According to Rhodes, et al., there was a trend to an increase in BMD with the exercising group, while there was a trend to a decrease in BMD with the control group.

This study brings up limitations that strength training has on BMD. Strength training can have a positive affect on BMD due to the mechanical loading and stress that it places upon the muscles and bones. However, the exercises must be intense enough to cause the bones to adapt. LaFontaine (1999) recommends intensities of *at least* 75% of 1-RM. Another limitation to strength training is that the proper exercises must be employed to have an affect on BMD. It is not enough to perform single-joint exercises such as arm curls, leg curls, leg extensions, etc. The bones must be loaded. This means multi-joint exercises such as squats, leg presses, lunges, and presses have to be used to have an affect on BMD.

There are a few other depressing things to keep in mind with exercise and BMD. First, exercise protocols are considered successful if they can slow down bone loss (i.e. instead of losing two percent per year one only loses one percent). Second, once it begins it is too late to stop bone loss even through exercise. This is depressing, but it is something that should kept in mind. The time to strengthen the bones is before bone loss begins. While exercise can help slow down bone loss from age, it is going to occur and starting out with greater bone mass means that one has more to lose.

CHANGES IN ENERGY USE AND STORAGE

Changes in the ability to use and store energy are specific to training. In other words, if one primarily trains to enhance the phosphagen energy system, then that is the system that will be enhanced through training.

Strength and conditioning is thought to enhance the resting levels of anaerobic substances (ATP, PC, creatine, and glyocen). This means there is more fuel on hand for intense exercise, allowing one to train with greater intensity for a greater duration. Exercise enhances the quantity and activation of the enzymes that control the anaerobic phase of glucose breakdown. Finally, exercise enhances the ability to generate and tolerate large levels of lactic acid. This means that you will be able to train harder for longer periods of time.

Strength training affects the development of a number of things in the human body. Muscle size increases, muscle shape changes, muscle strength increases, explosive strength increases, bones get stronger, and the ability to use and store energy is enhanced. These are not the only affects that strength training and conditioning has. Other affects may include (but are not limited to) endocrine/hormonal changes, changes in connective tissue strength, changes in joint range of motion, etc.

SAFETY AND STRENGTH TRAINING

With the complexity of the exercises and the weight that one can potentially lift, safety is a concern that many individuals have about strength training. Done properly, strength training is a safe and effective activity. Several studies have been done about safety and strength training. Zemper (1990), examined some ten thousand college football players over a four year period and found that there were 0.35 injuries in the weight room per 100 players per season. Most of the injuries he reported were either a result of the lifts being performed incorrectly or facility-related injuries. This underscores the importance of correct technique, proper set-up of a facility, and proper supervision.

With information like this in mind, this chapter is going to examine several broad categories that contribute to accidents/injuries in the weight room:

1. performance of the exercises,
2. lifting attire, and
3. equipment and facilities.

PERFORMANCE OF THE EXERCISES

Several things relating to the performance of the exercises could contribute to injuries. First, it is very important to perform the exercises correctly. Second, it is necessary to breath correctly while lifting weights. Third, when lifting weights one should observe proper back management. Finally, it is important to have attentive and knowledgeable spotters to help prevent injuries while lifting weights.

Proper Technique

Proper technique is an extremely important variable in preventing injuries. Failing to perform the exercises correctly could lead to the load being placed on muscles and structures it is not meant to be, which could lead to trauma or long-term overuse injuries. The chapters in this book on exercise techniques are designed to allow the reader to gain an understanding of proper exercise technique both to maximize performance and to prevent injuries.

Breathing

It is important to breathe while lifting weights. When one lifts weights, pressure builds up in the chest. Holding the breath shuts off the only escape valve that pressure has, this is known as the *Valsalva maneuver.* As a result of this, blood pressure can shoot up dramatically. For example, Zatsiorsky (1995) reports values of 320/250 mmHg during back squats. As a result of the Valsalva maneuver, cardiac output can decrease. The combination of increased blood pressure and decreased cardiac output can result in less oxygen reaching the brain. In other words, holding the breath while lifting weights can result in passing out.

Having said all that, there are exceptions to this rule. Participants in Olympic-style weightlifting and powerlifting frequently need to hold their breath while performing repetitions in order to maintain proper lifting posture. In addition, one will frequently need to hold his or her breath during a 1-RM test. There is a correct way to do this: if it is necessary to hold the breath while lifting weights, do so on each repetition *but not for the entire set.* In other words, hold the breath during the repetition, exhale, inhale, then perform the next repetition.

Proper Back Management

Back injuries from lifting weights typically come from bad technique. In Zemper's study, he found a total of thirty-eight time loss injuries from weight training. Forty percent of those were lower back injuries. Zemper hypothesized that those injuries were technique-related. Risser (1990) examined the literature and noticed that the bulk of weight-training related injuries were to the lower back. He also hypothesized that those injuries were due to poor technique.

When lifting an object from the ground, lifting it overhead, or squatting with it, an arched back posture should be used. This allows for the compressive load on the intervertebral disks to be placed on the muscles of the lower back, where it belongs. When an arched back posture is not used the pressure on the intervertebral disks and connective tissue is high and is not evenly distributed.

The arched back posture is referred to in this book as *setting the back.* In order to set the back, pull the shoulders back and elevate the chest. This should be an exaggerated posture. If this is done correctly, one should feel all the muscles along the spine tense up. This will be an uncomfortable feeling at first as those muscles get used to the posture.

Spotting

Spotting is important for many free-weight exercises. The primary purpose of spotting is injury prevention. On many exercises, spotting is also used to help the lifter to perform extra repetitions. Spotting is especially important with the following types of exercises:

1. over the face exercises (e.g. the bench press),
2. over the head exercises (e.g. behind the neck presses), and
3. squatting exercises.

Spotters should pay attention to the lifter that they are spotting, otherwise the lifter could end up seriously hurt. Spotters should ensure that the bar is loaded properly and that the weights don't slide off during the lift. They should be alert and use both hands when spotting. The sections of this book that discuss how to perform the various exercises also include sections on how to spot them.

Having discussed a little about the performance of the exercises and its role in injury prevention, it should be noted that this is only part of preventing injuries. Other causes of injuries can include lifting attire and equipment/facility issues.

LIFTING ATTIRE

Proper lifting attire is necessary for two major reasons, safety and courtesy. There are a number of recommendations regarding proper lifting attire. First, one should wear a shirt while exercising. This is important on exercises because sweat can make control of the barbell difficult. For example, when performing back squats, front squats, or good mornings; if one is not wearing a shirt and the shoulders and back are sweaty, then the barbell could slide off the back and shoulders potentially causing an injury. Sweat can also pool on benches and surfaces. Not only is this discourteous, but it can damage the naugahyde that covers many benches.

Wearing shoes is also extremely important when lifting weights. Proper footwear ensures a stable lifting base, which is especially important during squatting, lifting overhead, or lifting from the floor. Proper footwear also provides some protection from dropped weight plates, barbells, and dumbbells. Sandals and bare feet shout be avoided.

The final major contributing factor to safety and strength training concerns equipment and facility issues.

EQUIPMENT AND FACILITY ISSUES

When it comes to equipment and facilities, a number of situations can create an unsafe environment including equipment maintenance, supervision, overcrowding of people and equipment, and failing to put up equipment after use.

Equipment Maintenance

To prevent injuries, equipment maintenance must be done on a daily, weekly, and monthly basis. It is important to ensure that everything is working properly and, if not, that it is clearly labeled as being out of order.

	Daily	Weekly	Monthly	Quarterly
Clean Pads	X			
Clean Frames	X			
Re-Rack Loose Weights	X			
Bleach Barbells	X			
Lubricate Guide Rods		X		
Oil Barbells		X		
Inspect Cables and Handles		X		
Inspect Upholstery		X		
Clean & Lubricate Seat Post/Pin			X	
Clean & Lubricate Accessories			X	
Inspect All Clips/Collars			X	
Check Rotation			X	
Clean Weight Stacks				X
Clean Dumbbell Racks				X
Clean & Lube Inner Assembly				X

TABLE 3-1: Sample equipment maintenance list.

Surfaces that come into contact with skin should be cleaned and disinfected every day. Equipment should be lubricated and bolts/screws need to be checked often. Table 3-1 provides an overview of the preventative maintenance that can be done on strength training equipment.

Supervision

Supervision of lifting facilities has been cited as one of the major contributing factors to accidents during lifting. Supervision is essential to ensure that individuals are using the equipment correctly and safely. A lack of supervision can also be a liability problem.

Jones, et al. (2000) published a study that reviewed the data from emergency departments in hospitals across the country on weight training-related injuries over a twenty year span. They report a total of 980,173 people injured from weight training activity or equipment in those twenty years. Of those, 40% happened at home. They analyzed 97 cases in detail and report that 63% of the injuries studied occurred from unsafe behavior. This study underscores the need for proper supervision with weight training because typically individuals are not supervised by trained professionals at home.

Area	Items
Stretching, abdominal, and plyometric area	■ Weight benches and equipment should be away from area ■ Medicine balls, stability balls, abdominal equipment, stretching sticks, and stretching cords should be properly stored after use ■ Non-slip material on the top and bottom areas of plyometric boxes ■ Properly padded floor area below plyometric box area ■ Secure apparatus for holding feet for sit-ups and hyperextensions.
Free-weight area	■ Proper spacing of racks and weight trees to allow traffic flow and access ■ Return of all equipment after use to avoid obstructions ■ Nonslip mats on squat rack floor area ■ Nonslip surface on lifting platforms ■ Secure benches, weight racks, etc. to the floor or wall
Machine area	■ Easy access to each machine ■ Area free of clutter ■ Proper pins used for each machine ■ Free of all work parts (e.g. frayed cable, loose chains, etc.)

TABLE 3-2: Facility set-up suggestions. Adapted from Armitage-Johnson, S. (1990). Maintaining strength facility areas. *NSCA Journal, 12*(1), 25. Adapted with permission.

Overcrowding

Overcrowding of people or equipment can cause accidents. Too many people makes supervision difficult. It also increases the likelihood of traffic getting in the way of lifters, which can be dangerous to both parties. Having too much equipment in too little space can increase the likelihood of people bumping into equipment. Armitage-Johnson (1994a) recommends two to three feet of space in between machines. Table 3-2 has some recommendations about preventing equipment overcrowding and facility set-up.

An excellent source on administering, organizing, and running a strength and conditioning facility can be found on the National Strength and Conditioning Association's website. This document is called "*Strength and Conditioning Professional Standards and Guidelines*" and covers liability, staffing, supervision, etc. It can be located at: www.nsca-lift.org/Publications/standards.shtml.

Strength training can be a safe, rewarding activity. However, a number of factors need to be addressed by trainees and those people charged with maintaining/supervising the lifting facility to minimize injury risks. It is important that participants understand how to perform and spot the exercises correctly. It is important that trainees wear the proper clothing for lifting weights. Finally, it is important that the lifting facility is not crowded and that it is organized and maintained properly.

COMPONENTS OF A WORKOUT

It is important to have an understanding of what makes up strength and conditioning programs and how those programs are organized. Workouts typically have three main parts. They start with a beginning, which is designed to ease one gradually into the main workout. This beginning is called the *warm-up.* They have the main workout itself, this can be made up of one or more *modes of exercise* (i.e. types of exercise). The final part is the ending of the workout, which is designed to provide a transition between working hard and resting. This is called the *cool down.*
This chapter will be divided into the following sections:

1. the warm-up,
2. the modes of exercise, and
3. the cool down.

THE WARM-UP

The warm-up prepares the body for action. It is important for preventing injury and helping to maximize performance.
A warm-up prevents injury by increasing the temperature of the working joints and muscles. This is done through a number of mechanisms:

- redistribution of blood flow,
- muscle contractions, and
- the metabolism of fuels.

A properly performed warm-up will shunt blood from the skin and viscera to the muscles and connective tissue. This shunting of blood will help to increase the temperature of the muscles and connective tissue.
During the warm-up, the muscles will shorten and lengthen. The shortening and lengthening of the muscle fibers will cause friction, helping to increase the temperature in the muscles being exercised.
As was mentioned in chapter one, exercise (including the warm-up) will require the breaking down of substrates for fuel. The breaking down of substrates results in the release of heat which will further increase the temperature in the muscles.

Why is this increased temperature important for injury prevention? This is important because muscle elasticity and joint range of motion are dependent on temperature. As temperature increases so does the deformability of the muscle and joint. Think of the muscles as a rubber band, if the rubber band is at room temperature it is easy to stretch. However, if it is put in the freezer and frozen for a few hours, it will snap when one attempts to stretch it. The muscles and joints are working off the same principle.

A warm-up can also help to improve performance. This occurs through a number of mechanisms. First, a warm muscle will be able to contract more forcefully and relax faster than one that is not warm, which has implications for speed, strength, and power. Second, warming up helps to increase the ability of the nervous system to transmit messages, which can help with speed and reaction time. Third, by increasing temperature, the warm-up leads to more oxygen being available to exercising tissues. Finally, the warm-up allows one to practice the event by performing parts of the movement at lower intensities.

There are two parts to the warm-up:

1. *The general warm-up:* This part is designed to increase core and muscle temperature. It should be performed to the point of light sweating, it should not result in fatigue. Cardiovascular exercise, calisthenics, sprints, light plyometrics, and dynamic flexibility exercises are examples of exercises that are typically used in the general warm-up.

2. *The specific warm-up:* This part should fit the needs of the event or activity. It should follow the general warm-up (i.e. it should occur after the body's temperature has been raised). The specific warm-up is designed to focus on the body parts or movements that are to be used during the workout. Examples include medicine ball throws to warm up the upper body and core, jumping/sprinting exercises to warm up the lower body, technique exercises, etc.

Warming up should take 10-30 minutes. Well-trained athletes will need a more thorough warm-up than beginners due to the greater volume and intensity of an advanced athlete's training.

Table 4-1 shows some sample warm-ups for lifting weights. The table shows what area(s) the workout will emphasize (i.e. upper body, lower body, etc.). Then it provides a sample general warm-up that could be performed and a sample specific warm-up that could be performed. Note that everything is listed in the order in which it should be performed.

In both cases outlined in table 4-1, the general warm-up begins with some cardiovascular exercises. Upper body workouts focus on rowing because rowing uses the muscles of the upper body. After the cardiovascular exercise, dynamic flexibility and calisthenic exercises are thrown in to get the heart rate up and the blood flowing.

Workout Emphasis	General Warm-up	Specific Warm-up
Upper Body Weight Training	1. Cardiovascular exercise: rowing 5 minutes 2. Dynamic flexibility / calisthenics (2x10 yards or 2x10): a) Wheelbarrows b) Bear crawls c) Jumping jacks d) Mountain climbers e) Arm circles	1. Medicine ball exercises (3x5): a) Chest pass b) Overhead throws c) Behind body throw 2. Bench press, 3x6, light weights
Lower Body Weight Training	1. Cardiovascular exercise: stationary bicycle 5 minutes 2. Dynamic flexibility / calisthenics (2x10 yards or 2x10): a) Leg swings front/back b) Leg swings side/side c) Eagles d) Stomach eagles e) High knee walk f) Lunges, forward g) Lunges, side	1. Jumping exercises (3x5): a) Ankle hops b) Counter-movement jumps c) Squat jumps 2. Back squats, 3x6, light weight

TABLE 4-1: Examples of general and specific warm-ups for weight training.

The specific warm-up begins with exercises like medicine ball throws or jumping exercises that begin working the muscles and joints to be trained. The specific warm-up finishes with the first weight training exercise to be performed (bench press or back squat).

The warm-up needs to be fun and it needs to be directed towards the activities that will be performed. It is frequently one of the first things to be dropped when trainees view themselves to be pressed for time. It should never be dropped. The warm-up is important for the prevention of injuries and for the maximizing of performance.

What about stretching? Why isn't it in any of the warm-ups described? There is increasing evidence that stretching during the warm-up can actually decrease performance on strength and power activities and may actually increase the risk of injuries.

How could stretching increase one's potential of getting injured and decrease performance? Think back to the description of the warm-up at the beginning of this chapter. Stopping to perform static stretching will result in a number of things; first, heart rate will slow down. This means the amount of blood flow to the muscles will be reduced. Second, the muscles will not be contracting which means no fuel will be broken down and there will be no friction from the sliding of filaments. Reduced blood flow and reduced temperature will affect the supply of blood to the muscles and tissues. Muscles and ligaments will lose their elasticity, etc. As you can see, stopping a dynamic warm-up to perform a series of stretches will actually reverse everything that the warm-up has been trying to improve.

Once the trainee is warmed up, he or she is ready to begin the workout proper. But what should one do? Are any exercise types better than others? The next part of this chapter will discuss various modes of exercise in strength and conditioning workouts and some of the benefits and drawbacks of each.

THE MODES OF EXERCISE

There are several modes of exercise used in strength and conditioning workouts. One may train using only one mode or one may combine several. This chapter will cover the following modes of exercise:

1. free weights,
2. machine weights,
3. plyometrics, and
4. speed training.

Free Weights

Free weights refer to barbells and dumbbells. They have a number of benefits for a strength and conditioning program. First, they are thought to provide a greater transfer of training effect to athletic or ergonomic tasks than machine weights. This is due, in part, to the fact that they allow proprioceptive and kinesthetic feedback to occur in a manner similar to athletics or "real life." Free weights require the user to balance the barbell or dumbbells (thus involving more muscles in the exercise) and also allow for movements in many planes of motion. They allow for a great deal of exercise variation (e.g. hand spacing, foot spacing, etc.). Table 4-2 provides an example of the variations possible for the bench press exercise. Notice how small changes in the exercise can dramatically affect what the exercise develops. This is not possible with machine exercises. Barbell and dumbbells are also better for large-muscle / multi-joint training, which maximizes one's time in the weight room.

Free weights do have drawbacks. First, due to safety reasons one needs to have a spotter on certain exercises (see chapter three for more about this). In other words, it may be difficult to train alone effectively using free weights. Second, it takes time to learn the exercises. This may or may not be an efficient use of one's training time. Finally, machines (unlike free weights) provide for better isolation of specific joint angles and movements.

Machine Weights

Machine weight training exercises are easy to learn, possibly providing for a more efficient use of one's training time. They are safer, generally not requiring spotters. Machines are also better at isolating muscles, velocities, and motions.

Variation	Effects
Close grip hand spacing	Emphasizes triceps more, less stress on the rotator cuff
Wide grip hand spacing	Emphasizes pectoralis major more, bar travels less distance so more weight could be handled
Pause bench press	Exercise becomes more difficult to perform, develops strength off the chest
Reverse grip bench press	Emphasizes triceps
Eccentric-emphasis bench press	Exaggerated eccentric phase, helps lifter learn to lower the bar with control and develops explosiveness off the chest
Towel bench press	Emphasizes triceps more, less stress on the rotator cuff, develops strength on the lock-out

TABLE 4-2: Sample variations possible with the bench press exercise. Many of these are described in chapter ten.

However, unlike free weights only one or two exercises may be performed on a machine, which is not an efficient use of weight room space. Machines allow for little exercise variety and allow movement in only a single plane of motion (though there are some exceptions to this). As a result, proprioception and coordination is not developed. They are also more expensive than free weights.

Lifting with barbells, dumbbells, and machines are not the only way that strength and conditioning workouts may take place. Exercises may also use bodyweight or odd implements like medicine balls and kettle bells. In fact, some of these bodyweight or odd implement workouts may produce better speed/power gains than lifting with free weights and machines.

Plyometrics

Plyometrics are exercises that allow a muscle to reach maximum strength in as short a time as possible. They involve various types of jumps, hops, skips, bounds, throws, etc. Generally the goal is to perform the exercises as quickly and explosively as possible. According to Bompa (1994), plyometrics have the following benefits:

- they recruit most of the motor units in exercising muscles and their corresponding muscle fibers,
- they increase the firing rate of motor neurons,
- they transform maximum strength into explosive strength, and
- they develop the nervous system so that it reacts with maximal speed to the lengthening of the muscle, which in turn develops the ability to shorten rapidly and with maximal force.

How can plyometrics accomplish these things? They seek to take advantage of and train two physiological features in the human body, the *stretch reflex and elastic energy.*

Muscles have the ability to "sense" the rate of a stretch. When a muscle is stretched quickly, muscle spindles (located in series with the muscle fibers) send a message to the spinal cord. The spinal cord immediately relays a message back to the muscles telling them to shorten. This stretch reflex is meant to keep the muscles from stretching too quickly and thus getting injured.

When a muscle is stretched quickly it can store energy, when this fast stretch is immediately followed by a fast contraction it often results in additional force being generated.

Try this experiment and see when you can jump higher. Squat down until your thighs are parallel to the floor. Pause for ten seconds. Now, without dipping down jump straight up into the air. Now try it this way: quickly go down into a 1/4 squat. Without pausing, drive back up into the air. Chances are you will jump higher the second way. This is because of elastic energy. Most athletic events take advantage of this phenomenon in some manner.

Having seen some of the benefits and the science behind plyometrics, it is time to get into some specifics of employing plyometrics in a conditioning program. As with any workout program, it is important to warm-up before a plyometric workout. Chu (1998) recommends using jogging, skipping, footwork drills, lunges, and alternative movements (like running backwards) to help warm-up for plyometric workouts. Once one is warmed up, several different types of plyometric movements can be employed in a workout:

- jumps-in-place,
- throws,
- standing jumps,
- multiple hops and jumps,
- bounding,
- box drills, and
- depth jumps.

A jump-in-place is one where the jumper lands in the same place he/she started from. Throws involve implements such as medicine balls or kettle bells. Standing jumps stress a single, all-out effort either horizontally or vertically. Multiple hops and jumps are done one after the other. They can be performed without equipment or over barriers. Bounding exaggerates the normal running stride and helps to improve running techniques. Box drills incorporate both vertical (up onto the box) and horizontal (over the box) components. Depth jumps involve stepping off a box and dropping to the ground, then attempting to jump back up as high as possible.

It is crucial for the prevention of injuries that one progress slowly in plyometric training. One should start at the simplest version of the exercises (jumps-in-place and throws) and learn correct techniques before progressing to the next level. Not only does this ensure that the exercises are beneficial, it also prevents injuries that may result from bad technique or overtraining.

Chu (1998) recommends 48-72 hours of rest in-between plyometric sessions, generally no more than two sessions per week. He also recommends that these be done when the athlete is still fresh (i.e. not after an intense practice or weight workout). Very simple forms of plyometrics could be used as part of a warm-up for weight training, as we saw earlier in this chapter.

Plyometrics develop jumping ability (vertically or horizontally) and throwing. They can also be used to enhance running technique. While these are all important skills in athletics, realize that plyometrics do not do a good job of enhancing sprinting speed. To increase speed, one will have to perform speed workouts.

Speed Training

With regards to speed training, we are referring to exercises that train the ability to run fast over short distances (i.e. sprinting). Improving running speed is accomplished by improving a number of things:

- technique,
- stride length,
- stride frequency,
- acceleration,
- maximum velocity, and
- speed endurance.

Technique is important for preventing injuries and for maximizing performance. One of the major aspects of technique that should be observed is dorsiflexion when running. Athletes should keep their big toe pointed up at all times during sprinting and the ankle should be dorsiflexed to about 90 degrees. Athletes should sprint so that the ball of the foot contacts the ground in a pawing motion. If an athlete is sprinting in a heel-to-toe fashion then they will brake as they run - which is counterproductive to running fast! Running heel-to-toe will also aggravate hamstring and shin splint problems.

The foot should contact the ground slightly in front of the athlete's hips. As the hips travel over the foot, the athlete should plantarflex his/her ankle in preparation of pushing off the ground. As the foot breaks contact with the ground, it should immediately be "cast" (or dorsiflexed to 90 degrees) and the cast foot should be brought up to the athlete's hip. As the foot is brought to the hip, the hip will be flexed to approximately 45 degrees. This action serves to "shorten the lever" to allow the foot/leg to be swung forward more quickly.

As the foot is brought towards the hip, the foot/leg should be swung forward with the goal being to step over the opposite knee. After this is done, the thigh should be nearly parallel to the ground and the ankle should still be cast. The foot should be driven down to the ground from the hip so that the ball of the foot contacts the ground just in front of the athlete's hips.

Other technique cues relate to posture and arm action. Athletes should concentrate on keeping the hips tall, head should be level, shoulders should not be hunched, and the face and shoulders should be relaxed. With arm action, the arms should be moved forwards and backwards but never across the midline. Hands should be swung from the hips to the height of the shoulders. Elbows should be flexed at a loose 90 degrees while the hand is at shoulder level, the elbow should be allowed to open up to about 140 degrees when the arm is behind the body.

Stride length is the distance that each stride covers. To a point, taking longer strides will allow the athlete to cover a given distance faster. Care needs to be taken, however, when changing stride length because overstriding will cause a braking action and will fatigue the muscles used in sprinting faster than a normal stride length.

Stride frequency refers to how quickly the athlete moves his or her legs. The more foot contacts one can make in a given amount of time, the faster one can potentially run. Increasing this is accomplished by correct technique (i.e. dorsiflexion, bringing the heel to the hip, raising the knees high, using the arms as short and quick levers, etc.) and through special drills that are designed to get the athlete used to moving his/her limbs faster than normal.

The first 12-15 meters of a sprint are referred to as the *acceleration phase,* i.e. the phase during which the athlete's speed is rapidly increasing. It is important to distinguish because running mechanics are different over the first 12-15 meters. Because the athlete does not have the velocity and stride length that he/she would have at faster speeds, mechanics will focus on what happens in front of the body. In other words, the focus is on having a high knee, dorsiflexed ankle, driving the foot down from the hips, landing on the ball of the foot, etc. as opposed to what happens behind the body (heel to hip, cycle through, etc.). Acceleration is trained primarily using short sprints. After the first 12-15 meters, athletes transition into the full technique described above, though maximum speed will usually not be attained until the athlete has been running for six to seven seconds.

Maximum velocity refers to the maximum speed an athlete can attain. It may take a sprinter six to seven seconds to reach maximum velocity. Maximum velocity is trained using a number of tools. First, athletes can do sprints that are long enough to allow them to reach maximum velocity. Second, athletes can make the sprinting motion more difficult by running against resistance. Third, athletes can be assisted while sprinting thereby allowing them to move their limbs faster than is normally possible. Finally, athletes can perform sprints at variable speeds which will help teach the athlete to run relaxed.

Speed endurance refers to the ability to maintain speed over time. This is an important ability for many track athletes as the athlete who slows down the least may be the one who wins, particularly in longer events such as the 200 meter, 400 meter, and 800 meter sprints. This quality may not be relevant to many sports. Speed endurance is typically trained with longer sprints and careful manipulation of rest and recovery.

Speed workouts should be done while the athlete is fresh and should stress the appropriate energy system. It is important that sprinters are

Distance Run per Sprint	Number of Reps per Set	Rest in Between Reps	Number of Sets per Workout	Rest in Between Sets
20-80 meters	3–4	1.5–3 minutes	1–4	8–10 minutes
80-400 meters	1–5	2–10 minutes	1–4	10–20 minutes
300 meters–15 kilometers	3–20	1–3 minutes	1–4	5–8 minutes

TABLE 4-3: Recommendations for speed workouts. Adapted from Thompson, P.J.L. (1991). *Introduction to Coaching Theory.* Monaco: International Amateur Athletic Federation, pp. 2.20.

completely recovered in between sets. When sprinters are unable to run the sprints at the desired speed, or when fatigue causes technique to break down, the sprint workout should be stopped. Teaching athletes to sprint slowly and with terrible form is counter-productive. Table 4-3 provides basic recommendations for the number of sets, number of reps, rest in between reps, and rest in between sets for speed work of different distances.

Workouts should begin with a warm-up to help ease one into the workout. This prevents injuries and helps to improve performance. Then any one of several modes of exercise may be employed in the actual workout itself. As the workout begins winding down, one enters the final stage which is the cool down.

THE COOL DOWN

The cool down does not receive the same amount of attention in the literature as warming up and working out does. The cool down refers to a period of low-intensity activity that follows the workout and precedes cessation of the exercise session. The purpose of the cool down is to prevent injuries by providing a transition stage between high-intensity exercise and complete rest.

Single-joint exercises (e.g. "isolation" exercises) may be used as a cool down for a weight training workout (i.e. after complex, multi-joint exercises). Stretching may be used as a cool down following weight training. With sprinting or plyometrics, shin splint prevention drills and light jogging may be used as a cool down. Another activity that may be used as a cool down following workouts is a sports game. For example, 10 to 15 minutes of basketball after a workout could be a type of cool down. Not only can this be fun, but it can also teach movement skills that will help the athlete.

Strength and conditioning programs are made up of essentially three parts. The beginning, or warm-up, which prepares one mentally and physically for exercise. Next comes the main part, which is the workout itself. Depending upon needs and availability any one of several exercise modes may be employed in a conditioning workout. Each of these modes have their particular strengths, weaknesses, and benefits. Finally, a transition should be provided from exercise to rest. This transition which will help prevent soreness and may provide additional skills.

PRINCIPLES AND CONCEPTS IN PROGRAM DESIGN

A number of principles and concepts govern successful program design. These apply to the conditioning of all levels of athletes as well as to the general fitness population. Failure to observe these principles and concepts will make training much more difficult.

This chapter will cover the following principles and concepts:

1. specificity,
2. overload,
3. reversibility,
4. individualization,
5. exercise order, and
6. muscle balance.

SPECIFICITY

The principle of specificity states that the nature of training will determine the training effects. When discussing athletics, this principle refers to how well conditioning translates into improved performance. The closer conditioning exercises resemble the event they are enhancing, the stronger the transfer effects between the two will be.

When designing strength and conditioning programs for athletes, the principle of specificity requires that you keep a number of factors in mind:

1. What energy systems supply the event?
2. What major muscle groups and joint motions contribute to the event?
3. At what velocity is the event performed?
4. What is the athlete's training status?

What Energy Systems Supply the Event?

When it comes to energy systems, you should have an idea of what limits the performance of the sport/event for which you want to train. By knowing this, you can manipulate your training so that it enhances this aspect.

For example, if you were training to become a better shot putter you should know that the shot put lasts seconds. This means that the bulk of the energy supplying the activity will be from the phosphagen energy system (i.e. ATP/PC). Therefore, training needs to be performed in a way that enhances ATP/PC supplies, in other words heavy weights and few repetitions.

In something a little more complicated like basketball, you would need to develop both the phosphagen energy system and the lactic acid energy system. Training would need to focus on brief, explosive training and on longer training with brief rest periods.

What Major Muscle Groups and Joint Motions Contribute to the Event?

The selection of specific exercises should be dictated by an analysis of the muscles and joint actions involved in the activity. Many sports have running, jumping, pushing, and throwing in common. These skills involve the muscles of the abs, low back, lower body, and upper body to some degree. These skills require an athlete to exert force from the ground with many muscle groups working together. As a result, the exercises employed in a conditioning program should be:

    a) ground-based,

    b) multi-joint, and

    c) have a core and lower-body emphasis.

At What Velocity is the Event Performed?

Strength training is believed to be velocity specific. According to Behm and Sale (1993), the greatest increase in strength occurs at or near the velocity of the training exercise. Others have found that strength increases at the speeds one trains or at slower speeds. In other words, if you train slowly then you will be slow.

The exception to this rule is with untrained athletes. In untrained athletes, simply increasing maximum strength (i.e. with slow exercises) seems to be enough to increase explosive strength. However, in highly trained athletes this does not hold true.

What is the Athlete's Training Status?

In highly trained athletes, all aspects of specificity (especially velocity) are extremely important. If you are out of shape, or have never trained, then any conditioning will improve your performance. However, high level athletes will have very different conditioning needs. This will be discussed in more detail in the next chapter.

What does specificity actually look like when it is applied to athletes? How does it differ with beginning versus high level athletes? Table 5-1 is meant to compare the differences between a beginning 100-meter sprinter and a high-level 100-meter sprinter.

Aspects of Specificity	Beginning Sprinter	High-Level Sprinter
Energy System	■ Event takes approximately 10 seconds ■ Amount of ATP/PC on hand will limit performance	■ Event takes approximately 10 seconds ■ Amount of ATP/PC on hand will limit performance
Muscle Groups/Joints	Particular attention should be paid to the: ■ Hip flexors ■ Hamstrings ■ Dorsiflexors ■ Plantar flexors ■ Core muscles. ■ Ground-based exercises ■ Multi-joint exercises	Particular attention should be paid to the: ■ Hip flexors ■ Hamstrings ■ Dorsiflexors ■ Plantar flexors ■ Core muscles. ■ Ground-based exercises ■ Multi-joint exercises
Velocity of training	■ Develop base by developing slow strength ■ Perform some high velocity strength training	■ Most training should be high velocity ■ Some slow strength training to maintain base strength

TABLE 5-1: Differences between beginning and advanced sprinters with regards to specificity of training.

As you can see, the major difference deals with the velocity of the training exercises that both will employ.

If you are not concerned with athletics, but are more interested in fitness or bodybuilding, then specificity will still apply to your training. Here are some things to consider when it comes to specificity:

a) Why are you training? Are you training to improve something concrete and measurable or for a concept?

b) If you are training to improve something concrete and measurable, then:

1) What energy systems supply the event?

2) What major muscle groups and joint motions contribute to the event?

3) What velocity is the event performed at?

For example, if you are concerned about how much weight you can bench press one time, then the phosphagen energy system will be the one to provide the energy for that activity. With that in mind you would need to organize a training program that develops that energy system. In other words, your training program would need to include heavier weights, with fewer repetitions per set. A maximal bench press will emphasize the muscles of the chest, shoulders, and triceps and will require some upper back strength to assist with lowering the barbell. As a result those muscle groups will need to be stressed in training in a way that enhances the phosphagen energy system. Finally, a maximal bench press will be a slow, controlled activity. This means that the muscles of the chest, shoulders, triceps, and upper back will need to be trained in a way that is slow and controlled but enhances the phosphagen energy system.

For another example, if you were trying to improve how many sit-ups you could perform in two minutes, you will need to know that the body's ability to deal with large levels of lactic acid will limit your performance in sit-ups. The abdominal and hip flexor muscles are heavily involved in this activity, so they will need to be trained in a way that enhances their ability to deal with lactic acid (i.e. high repetitions with little rest). Finally, to do well on the sit-up test you will almost have to perform a sit up per second, which means that the muscles of the abdominals and hip flexors need to be trained in a way that enhances their ability to contract very quickly.

If you are training for a concept, then you must consider what is required to make that concept happen. For example:

1. *Hypertrophy:* When training for hypertrophy, you are training to make your muscles larger. Not counting warm-up sets, this is done by performing three to five sets an exercise. Each set should be done with 8-12 repetitions. You should only get 30-60 seconds of rest between each set. When training for hypertrophy, you don't want to give your muscles a chance to fully recover between each set. This makes them grow in order to keep performing the work. Generally, when training for hypertrophy you are primarily training the lactic acid system, with some help from the phosphagen system.

2. *Strength:* When training for strength, you are trying to make your muscles stronger. Not counting warm-up sets, this is done by performing three to five sets an exercise. Each set should be done with three to nine repetitions. You may also take as long as three to five minutes between each set. When you are training for strength, the idea is to let your muscles recover fully before attempting to lift the heavy weights again. Generally, training for strength concentrates on the phosphagen energy system (i.e. heavy weight, few reps) and to some extent the lactic acid system.

3. *Endurance:* When training for endurance you are training to do more of something (i.e. more sit-ups, more dips, etc.). This is done by performing at least three sets an exercise. Each set is done with at least 12 repetitions. Also, you should only give yourself around 30 seconds of rest between each set. The idea behind training for endurance is to train the body to withstand larger levels of lactic acid, therefore the training has to be very fast paced.

Ensuring that training is set up to address the specific needs of an activity or goal is a necessary step in getting the desired outcome from working out. Another important step in getting the desired outcome from working out is making sure that the workouts are difficult enough.

OVERLOAD

The overload principle states that training adaptations take place only if the magnitude of the training load is above the habitual load. In other words, fitness only increases when the exercises are difficult enough to force an adaptation. According to Zatsiorsky (1995), training loads may be:

1. *Stimulating:* the training is enough to cause an adaptation. For example, if you normally squat 135 pounds ten times and then you start squatting 155 pounds ten times, that would be an example of making your workouts more difficult and forcing an adaptation (i.e. you get stronger and your leg muscles may grow).

2. *Retaining:* the training is enough to maintain your fitness, but not enough to make you improve your fitness. The drawback to this approach is that if an athlete's training does not improve over time, then neither will his or her results in sports. In fact, results will decrease. This is due to the *principle of accommodation.* This principle states that the response of a biological object to a given constant decreases over time. In other words, simply performing the same workouts day after day, even if they were difficult at first, will eventually lead to your losing fitness!

3. *Detraining:* if the training magnitude is too low, then detraining will occur. For example, if you can lift 100 pounds, but instead elect to work out with 20 pounds, you will eventually lose strength and muscle mass.

How does one insure that training remains stimulating? By applying *progressive overload.* Progressive overload states that training must be increased regularly for performance to improve. This is accomplished by changing training loads or changing the exercises.

Changing the training loads refers to increasing volume and/or intensity. *Volume* is the quantity of the work one performs (i.e. sets and reps) while *intensity* is the quality of the work done (i.e. amount of weight, percentage of maximum, speed, etc.). Increasing the difficulty of the exercises by increasing the resistance or by increasing the amount performed will keep training stimulating. However, specificity must still be observed when changing the training loads.

For example, the 100 meter sprinter was performing the following workout before things became more difficult:

1. Power Snatch, 3x3x75%

2. Clean Pull, 3x6x80%

3. Back Squats, 3x8x80%

4. Lying Leg Curls, 3x12-RM

Volume: 87 repetitions, Average Intensity: 79.12% of 1-RM

To apply the overload principle correctly, you need to keep in mind that the sprinter needs to develop his phosphagen energy system (i.e. short bursts of activity) and his speed of movement. As a result, the repetitions have to be kept fairly low. The only exception to that is in the muscles of the lower body where we'd like some hypertrophy to occur. So, after applying the overload principle the new workout will look like this:

1. Power Snatch, 3x3x77.5%
2. Clean Pull, 3x6x82.5%
3. Back Squats, 3x10x80%
4. Lying Leg Curls, 3x10-RM

Volume: 87 repetitions, Average Intensity: 80.39% of 1-RM

The amount of weight used on the power snatch, clean pull, and lying leg curls has been increased and the number of repetitions used on the back squats has been increased. Overall volume is maintained (though it is different on back squats and leg curls) whereas average intensity is increased. Specificity is observed.

Changing the exercises is another way to apply the overload principle. Provided that specificity is observed, this will keep training stimulating. Changing the exercises will change the muscles recruited during training and the way in which those muscles are recruited. By modifying the stimulus you will force the muscles to continue to adapt to training.

Going back to the hypothetical sprinter. If intensity and volume remained the same, but the exercises employed were changed, specificity would still need to be observed. It is going to be important to use explosive exercises (i.e. Olympic lifting movements) as well as lower body exercises. So, the new workout might look like this:

1. Power Snatch from the hang, bar at knee height
2. Power Clean
3. Front Squats
4. Standing Leg Curls

Two explosive exercises are still included, a squat is still included, and an exercise for the hamstrings is still included.

How often should training be evaluated and modified to observe the overload principle? Constantly! This will be discussed in more detail in the next chapter, but periodization and some of the other training approaches, done properly, attempt to make sure that this happens.

Training needs to be constantly evaluated so that it remains stimulating. Failure to do so can cause you to regress rather than to progress. This is due to the principle of reversibility.

REVERSIBILITY

As was indicated in the section on overload, you can detrain. This is because the gains from exercise are reversible. If you do not continue to exercise, or if you do not do so at a level that will cause overload, you will eventually lose the gains you have made through exercise.

Specificity, overload, and the fact that exercise is reversible are all important concepts to keep in mind when designing a program. Also important is the realization that we are all different and unique.

Individualization

This principle states that everyone is different and will react to a given training stimulus differently. It is not enough to simply copy someone else's workout programs. As will be demonstrated in the next chapter, programs should be about addressing an individual's specific needs, deficiencies, history, and current training status. Simply copying a champion's program may result in some gains, but it may also result in injury or no gains. It is better to learn the why's behind programs and adapt them to fit you and your needs.

One key concept in learning the why's behind strength and conditioning programs is understanding how to organize the exercises.

Exercise Order

The order of the exercises will affect how the workout is experienced. Those lifts requiring the largest muscle groups (i.e. total body or legs) should be done first, followed by lifts using the smaller muscle groups. This is because those lifts using the largest muscle groups require the most energy and technique to perform, so they should be done while the lifter is still fresh.

To help you determine how to order your exercises, consider the following. First, perform the total body exercises. Second, look at what is involved in the main exercises you are performing.

When you are pushing using the upper body, you can use your chest to push the bar (as during the bench press). However, whenever you use your chest, you also use your shoulders and triceps to help your chest push. When you are pushing, you could push just using your shoulders (i.e. like when you perform a behind the neck press). However, whenever you use your shoulders to push you also use your triceps to help your shoulders. You could also push by just using your triceps (during a triceps extension for example). Therefore, using this logic you can see that the triceps are the most easily isolated muscle group in this chain. Because they are the weakest and most easily isolated group, they should be trained last. The shoulders are the next most-easily isolated group, so they should be trained second. The chest is the strongest and most difficult to isolate muscle group, so it should be trained first- because any chest pushing movement will involve using the shoulders and triceps. If you were to train every muscle group in the same session, a recommendation for how to organize your exercises would be:

1. total body lifts,
2. multi-joint leg exercises such as squats, leg presses, and RDL's,
3. single-joint leg exercises such as leg extensions and calf raises,

4. multi-joint chest exercises such as bench presses, incline presses, and dips,

5. single-joint chest exercises such as flies *OR* multi-joint upper back exercises such as rows, pull ups, and pull downs,

6. multi-joint shoulder exercises such as military presses, behind the neck presses, and upright rows *OR* biceps exercises,

7. single-joint shoulder exercises such as lateral raises, and

8. triceps exercises.

Knowing how to organize the exercises is necessary to make your workouts effective. Making certain that you include the proper exercise so that everything is trained in balance is another key step.

MUSCLE BALANCE

Muscle balance refers to the strength ratios between opposing muscle groups (e.g. biceps and triceps, hamstrings and quadriceps, etc.). Muscle balance is a concept used in the prevention of injuries from long-term training. It is important to train all the muscles around a joint. Failure to do so could cause a strength imbalance leading to injury.

An example of the importance of muscle balance is distance running. Running is primarily a hamstring activity. As a result of this, the quadriceps get little training from distance running. The strength imbalance that develops from this is thought to be one cause of knee injuries in runners.

A word of caution about muscle balance and strength ratios, the exact strength ratio between opposing muscle groups that would be considered "safe" or "ideal" is hard to pin down. This is because most of the testing that has developed these norms has been done in conditions that do not necessarily duplicate real life activities. Most of this testing has been done at certain speeds (using isokinetic equipment) and at certain joint angles. As a result, many of the reported "ideal" ratios may only be valid under those testing conditions.

Designing strength and conditioning programs boils down to a number of concepts and ideas. First, train for what you want. Second, make sure your workouts are difficult enough to make gains. Along with that, it is important to progressively make your workouts harder over time. Third, if you do not use it, you will lose it. Fourth, you are an individual, so my workout program will not have the same results for you. Fifth, the most difficult and most complex exercises need to be performed at the beginning of a workout, while you are still fresh. Finally, make sure to keep your training balanced. By keeping those six concepts in mind you will greatly improve your odds of getting the results you want from a strength and conditioning program.

PERIODIZATION OF TRAINING

According to Freeman (1994), periodization is an attempt to make the training process more objectively measurable, thus more accurately planned and evaluated along the way to a more reliable peak. Periodization applies progressive overload to training by systematically manipulating volume, intensity, exercise selection, exercise order, frequency of training, and rest/recovery. According to Gambetta (1991a) periodization allows one to:

1. identify problem areas,
2. separate the need to do from the want to do,
3. prepare for optimal performance improvement,
4. prepare for a peak or climax to training,
5. ensure the long-term development of an athlete, and
6. develop a fitness base in athletes by advancing from general training to specific training.

The first step in designing a long-term program for an individual is to determine where that individual is deficient. This is necessary so that we may identify what needs to be improved.

Identifying Problem Areas

Ideally, periodization is a process which calls for a constant evaluation of the athlete's fitness and training status. Testing should occur regularly in order to identify deficiencies and also to provide feedback on the effectiveness of the training program.

For example, if we are working with a wide receiver there are a number of characteristics we'd want to see developed: running speed, jumping height, ability to change directions quickly, upper body strength, and lower body strength. So in addition to keeping track of the volume and intensity from training, we can also select tests that evaluate each of those qualities listed above and keep track of them during the course of training.

Once an individual's deficiencies have been identified they can be prioritized. Many athletes would like to have big biceps, but is that necessary? Should precious training time be devoted to that? This is where decisions must be made about what is important and what is necessary.

Separating the Need to Do from the Want to Do

Periodization's systematic nature requires a coach and athlete to prioritize and focus on what is important. There are not enough hours in the day to develop everything. There is also a very real danger of overdoing things and thus decreasing an athlete's performance. By prioritizing and planning things out, one can help prevent overtraining by focusing on what is important and ignoring what is not.

Once weaknesses have been identified and it has been determined what needs to be addressed through training, it is time to put the training program together to make success happen.

Preparing for Optimal Performance Improvement

Periodization prepares for optimal performance improvement. If an athlete's training does not improve over time then neither will his or her performance. By quantifying training, periodization provides a way to safely increase volume and intensity over time, leading to long-term increases in the athlete's fitness levels.

In a periodized program there needs to be a focus for the training. The athlete is meant to be at his or her physical best during this focus. It might be a block of time (e.g. football season) or a single event (e.g. the Olympic Games).

Preparing for a Peak or Climax to the Training

A periodized program is designed to ensure the athlete is at his or her best when it counts, in competition. In periodization, variables are carefully manipulated to raise the athlete's fitness level until it is at its highest point for the competition(s). Running a PR the week after the Olympic Games will not do any good!

Traditional periodization programs involve gradual changes in volume and intensity as the training cycle progresses. Typically intensity will increase as one gets closer to the season and volume will decrease as one gets closer to the season. This means that athletes typically use the heaviest weights with the smallest volume during the season.

Periodization attempts to organize long-term (multi-year) training so that athletes have the fitness and motor-skill base they need to achieve optimum sports performance.

Ensuring the Long-Term Development of the Athlete

By carefully and methodically increasing the athlete's fitness over time, periodization seeks to insure that athletes do not become overly specialized too early in their careers. This will keep them from reaching their long-term potential and may cause burn-out and injury.

With multi-year approaches to training, athletes start out using very general approaches to fitness. They work on developing many motor skills such as running, jumping, throwing, kicking, endurance, strength, power, etc.

Year	Volume (number of lifts)	Intensity (average weight lifted in kilograms)	Best total (snatch + clean and jerk) for the year in kilograms
1974	6740	100	255
1975	9784	104	297
1976	11803	113	340
1977	12272	126	355
1978	16000	128	370
1979	20000	136	390
1980	15000	140	400
1981	20000	142	415
1982	17188	145	422

TABLE 6-1: An example of multi-year changes in volume, intensity, and results. Adapted from Medvedyev, A.S. (1986). *A System of Multi-Year Training in Weightlifting.* Translated by Charniga, Jr. A. Livonia, Michigan: Sportivny Press. Adapted with permission.

As athletes get older they begin to perform less general work and focus on more specific work. In other words, as they get older they focus more on their specific sport. Many authorities feel that specializing in a particular sport too early will result in the athlete being unable to reach his or her potential.

By developing a solid base and by the systematic approach to training, periodization seeks to ensure that one steadily improves performance over time. Note however, that this improvement will not be linear.

For example, Victor Sots was a world champion and world record holder in the 100 kilogram class in weightlifting from 1978 to 1982. Table 6-1 shows how his average intensity of weight lifted (in kilograms), the volume (number of lifts) of his training, and his total (snatch + clean and jerk) changed from 1974 to 1982.

As can be seen from the table, volume, intensity, or both, increase from year to year but not at a constant rate. Competition results also increase from year to year, but not at a constant rate. Figure 6-1 also serves to demonstrate how volume and intensity may change from year to year, but not at a constant rate. This example serves to underscore the fact that strength trainees will not improve at a constant rate over time.

Periodization is useful for the long-term development of athletes. It also prepares athletes to be at their best in competition by moving them from "general" training at the beginning of the cycle to more "specific" training as competition nears.

Developing a Fitness Base by Advancing From General Training to Specific Training

Periodization seeks to increase performance by developing a strong fitness base. This is traditionally accomplished by progressing an athlete through several phases of training: general preparation to special preparation to competition to a transitional phase. Each phase has different objectives.

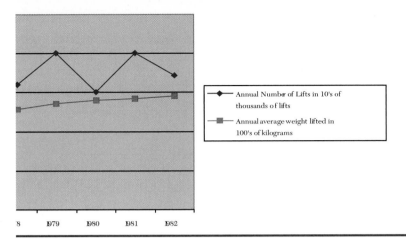

FIGURE 6-1: Intensity and Volume over time for Victor Sots, 1974–1982

The *General Preparation* phase of training (GPP) is designed to build a movement and fitness base. In this phase all aspects of fitness and sport are developed. Athletes will develop hypertrophy, strength, speed, power, and endurance. This phase generally lasts from eight to sixteen weeks.

Hypertrophy is necessary because larger muscles are potentially stronger muscles. Stronger muscles have the potential to be more explosive muscles. This phase serves to build a base for future, heavier, weight training. The hypertrophy training is also necessary to give joints and connective tissue a chance to adapt to training before the loads are increased. In other words, some hypertrophy is necessary because it potentially improves one's results later on and helps to prevent injury. Volume is higher in the GPP, generally 8-15 repetitions. Intensity is moderate in this phase of training, 70-85% of 1-RM depending on the exercise, the athlete's level of development, and where in the phase the athlete is.

Endurance is important in this phase because (within limits) improving endurance will enhance one's ability to recover from workouts. This is not to say that throwers or football players need to be running marathons during this phase. They can focus on higher repetitions (say 12-15) on certain exercises with little rest in order to build up their ability to recover from very difficult workouts.

The *Special Preparation* phase of training (SPP) is designed to take the fitness that was developed in GPP and apply it directly to the sport. This is where sport-specific training and drills really come into play. For most athletes this means focusing on strength and power (power especially as one moves further into this phase). Since the athlete developed the joints, connective tissue, and muscles in the last phase the intensity is increased (i.e. heavier weights) while the volume is decreased (i.e. fewer repetitions). Volume is lower in this phase of training, 4-12 repetitions would be a good guideline. Intensity is also higher in this phase of training, 75-90% of 1-RM depending on the exercise, the athlete's level of development, and where in the phase the athlete is. Generally the number of weight training sessions are cut back, their increased difficulty requires more recovery time than in the GPP. In addition, more time should be spent on sports skills, so less time should be available for weight training. This phase generally lasts four to eight weeks.

The *Competition* phase of training is the season. This is where the athlete should be at his or her peak. Less time should be available for training due to the rigors of competing and working on sports skills. This means that only the most important exercises should be included in training. It also means that this is typically the heaviest training of the season. Weights are heavy, many explosive exercises are included to peak power, and there should be fewer training sessions to allow for enhanced recovery. Volume is low in this phase, generally 1-8 repetitions. Intensity is very high in this phase, often 80-100% of 1-RM. This phase lasts the entire season.

The *Transitional* phase of training allow one a chance to recover from the previous phases of training. Training does not stop during the transitional phases, however it is altered in an attempt to use exercise to help the athlete recover mentally and physically. Exercises should be fun, new, infrequent (2-3 times per week), and should not be heavy. Things like games and medicine ball circuits would be great for a transitional phase of training. The point is to maintain fitness by doing something, but not to continue doing those things which the athlete has done in the previous training. This phase lasts two to four weeks.

When it comes to training, periodization allows one to do a number of things. First, it allows one to identify the problem areas. Second, it helps the coach and athlete to separate the need to do from the want to do. It prepares the athlete for optimal performance improvement and a peak or climax to the training. It ensures the long-term development of the athlete and develops a fitness base in athletes by advancing from general training to specific training. The combination of these allows for more effective training, safer training, and training that makes a more efficient use of an athlete's time. The rest of this chapter will cover the principles that periodization is based upon and cover the most popular approaches to periodization.

PRINCIPLES OF PERIODIZATION

The broad strokes of periodization were developed in the 1930's and 1940's and were systematized in Matveyev's book in the 1960's. Other authors have adapted and modified Matveyev's ideas over the years, including Bompa, Harre, Kurz, and Stone. No matter the author, each approach to periodization has several things in common. According to Matveyev (1981) and Bompa (1999), there are twelve principles that govern periodization. These include:

- Maximize individual achievement: not only should athletes perform at their best, but they should do so when it is important. Peaking two weeks after the Olympic games won't do an athlete any good. Periodization is designed to get athletes at their best when it is necessary.

- Active and conscientious participation in training: ultimately it is up to the athlete to execute the plan and perform. This means that the athlete has to be an active participant not only in training but also in the planning process, the athlete should understand what is being done and why and he or she should apply themselves to the training.

- Multilateral development: the idea behind multilateral development is the better well-rounded an athlete is in terms of physical skills and in terms of fitness, the faster he or she will master new skills and the faster he or she will recover from the training process.

- Sports specialization: at a certain point, athletes have to specialize and devote themselves to the given sport. At a certain point in the periodized year, the training needs to become much more specialized to focus on the specific needs of the sport.

- Individualization: everyone is an individual and this should be taken into account in the training process.

- Unity of general and special preparation: training needs to have a purpose and should relate to the rest of the training that will be done that year.

- Variety: ultimately training, especially over years, can become a boring grind. This is why variety is important, to keep the athletes challenged and interested.

- Model the training process: leave nothing to chance! What is needed for success in a given sport? Once that has been determined design the training to achieve that.

- Continuity of training: training is a long-term process and every training session should build on the one that came before it.

- Progressively increase the load in training: if the athlete is not getting better then they are falling behind the competition. Training should be carefully and progressively increased to help maximize performance while preventing injuries and overtraining.

- Cyclical nature of training: in most periodization models, training is a cyclical process that gradually builds up until the athlete peaks and then backs off and starts all over again.

- Supercompensation: forms the foundation of most periodization models. Training leads to fatigue and a temporary loss of fitness due to fatigue. Over time the system will restore and be a little stronger than before the workout. If training is timed properly, then supercompensation will be optimal (fitness will be increased). If training is not timed properly then supercompensation will not occur as fatigue will lead to a fitness decrease or will only lead to a maintenance of fitness. This is why most training programs are organized into a series of steps (for example, increase the intensity over 2-3 weeks then have a week of reduced intensity to allow for recovery).

No matter the author, periodization can be summarized as a way to organize training over the months and years that is designed to improve performance and prevent injuries. It is a procedure that is leading to something and also is a process that allows one to check if the training is producing the desired results. It is not a four to eight week long workout program, it is more than varying sets and repetitions, and is very difficult to implement in personal training situations while still adhering to the principles.

As we indicated earlier, several authors have written texts on periodization of training. The various approaches and texts makes this a confusing concept. The next part of this chapter will cover some of the more popular approaches and attempt to explain the major differences between the various approaches.

APPROACHES TO PERIODIZATION

There are several authors whose approach to periodization that this chapter will cover:

1. Matveyev,
2. Bompa,
3. Stone, and
4. Verkoshansky.

Matveyev and Periodization

Matveyev's book, *Fundamentals of Sports Training* was translated for the West in 1981. Matveyev observed the training of Soviet Olympic athletes as they prepared for the 1952 and 1956 Olympic games. He formalized the training process that he observed and this process is what is detailed in his book.

Matveyev divides exercises into three types; competitive, special preparation, and general preparation. Competitive exercises are those that contain integral actions; the competition exercises proper and the training forms of the competitive exercises. Special preparation exercises include elements or properties of the competitive exercises. General preparation exercises develop all physical qualities, they form the foundation for all training. For example, an Olympic-style weightlifter competes in the full (squat) snatch. The full snatch, the full snatch from the hang, and the full snatch from blocks would all be competitive exercises as they include the contested exercise and training forms of it. The power snatch, snatch pulls, and overhead squats would be examples of special preparation exercises that include elements or properties of the full snatch. Presses, squats, and Romanian deadlifts would be examples of general preparation exercises to help develop all the physical qualities necessary for the full snatch.

Matveyev structures the training process as follows:

1. Microcycles that consist of training sessions that make up a complete, recurrent fragment. Matveyev's more common types of microcycles include ordinary training, shock, introductary (aka pre-competition), competition, and rehabilitative. These are generally characterized by a constant intensity (i.e. an entire microcycle might be performed at 80% with sets of 8-12 repetitions) and an inverse relationship between volume and intensity (i.e. as intensity increases, volume decreases and vice versa).

2. Mesocycles that are an aggregate of several microcycles of one type and allow one to realize the sum effect of the microcycles. The most common organization of microcycles within a mesocycle are:

Ordinary - Ordinary - Shock - Rehabilitative

This means that there are three steps up (i.e. three increases in intensity) followed by one step down (the rehabilitative microcycle). Another way to write this is to say that this mesocycle has a 3:1 loading structure.

Matveyev lists several basic types of mesocycles:

■ Involving mesocycle: generally the first phase of the preparatory period. Low intensity, high volume, the biggest share of the general preparation exercises. Generally 2-3 ordinary microcycles and one rehabilitative microcycle (figure 6-2 is a sample of an involving mesocycle).

■ Base mesocycle: the main type seen in the preparatory period. Generally 1-2 ordinary microcycles, 1-2 shock microcycles, and 1 rehabilitative microcycle. Figure 6-3 is a sample of a

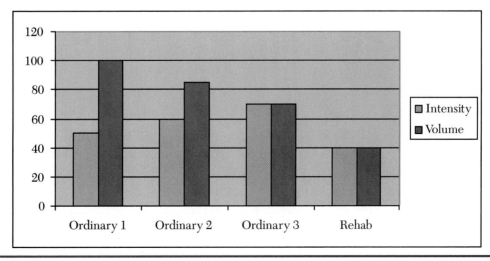

FIGURE 6-2: Sample involving mesocycle. First three microcycles (ordinary 1-3) involve steady increases in intensity and decreases in volume, the final microcycle (rehab) is a low intensity/low volume microcycle.

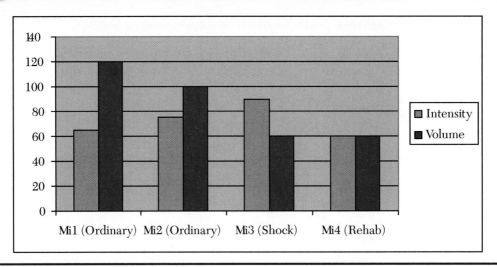

FIGURE 6-3: Sample base mesocycle, including two ordinary microcycles (Mi1 and Mi2), a shock microcycle (Mi3), and a rehab microcycle (Mi4).

base mesocycle. Notice that it begins with two ordinary microcycles, followed by a shock microcycle, and ends with a rehab mcrocycle.

■ Control-prep mesocycle: serves as a transition between the preparation and the competition phases. Higher intensity, lower volume, special preparation exercises. Generally consists of 1-2 ordinary or shock microcycles and 2 competitive microcycles.

■ Pre-competition mesocycle: may consist of some ordinary, shock, and competitive microcycles. Higher intensity, lower volume, special preparation and competitive exercises.

■ Competitive mesocycle: will consist of high intensity and low volume, mostly competitive exercises.

■ Rehabilitative mesocycle: rest and recovery, low volume and low intensity.

3. Macrocycles are designed to peak the athlete. There may be macrocycles with a single peak, two peaks, or three peaks. Macrocycles consist of mesocycles organized into three periods:

■ Preparation Period: Develops all the qualities needed for success. Makes up the bulk of the year. May last between three and seven months depending upon the number of peaks. Figure 6-4 provides an example of a six-month preparation period. Notice that volume is steadily decreasing while intensity is steadily increasing.

■ Competition Period: Includes the time spent preparing for competition and the competition(s). This is the peak, may last between one and a half and five months depending upon the number of peaks.

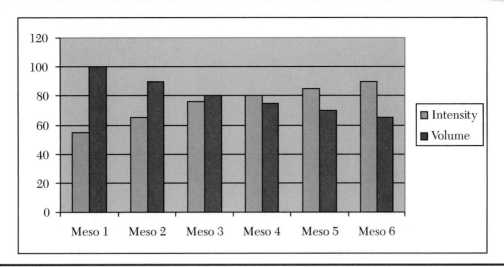

FIGURE 6-4: Sample six month preparation period. Period is done over six mesocycles, notice that intensity is steadily increasing as volume is decreasing.

■ Transition Period: Rest and recovery after competition. May last between three and six weeks depending upon the number of peaks.

Generally macrocycles are put together so that intensity is increasing over time while volume is decreasing. The competition period sees the highest intensity and the lowest volume. Figure 6-5 provides a sample macrocycle consisting of all three periods. Notice the trends in intensity and volume.

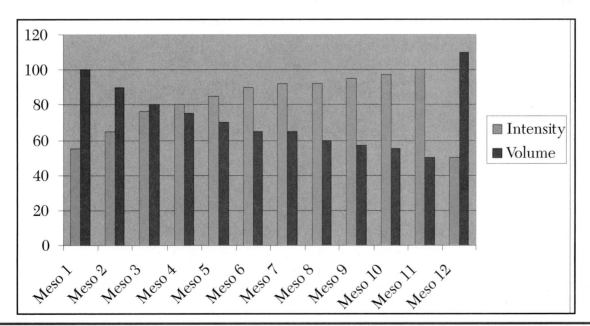

FIGURE 6-5: Sample 12-month macrocycle, done over twelve mesocycles. Mesocycle 1-7 represent the preparation period, mesocycles 8-11 represent the competition period, mesocycle 12 represents the transition period.

While widely used and quoted from, Matveyev's approaches have been criticized. First, these concepts were based on the preparation of the 1952 and 1956 Olympic athletes, training has progressed greatly in the last fifty years. This means that many of these concepts may be outdated. Second, a common criticism is that many of the principles, rules, and structure are arbitrary and are not based upon science. In fact, a common argument is that the structure behind Matveyev's approach actually interferes with an athlete's ability to improve over time and peak for competition. Finally, it may be impractical to apply these concepts outside of the carefully controlled society that they were developed in.

Bompa and Periodization

Tudor Bompa wrote *Theory and Methodology of Training*, which as of this writing is in its fourth edition. With Tudor Bompa's approach to periodization, the terminology is used a little differently than with Matveyev, sometimes making reading the two confusing. Bompa uses the following terms in his structuring of the training process:

- Microcycles
- Macrocycles: aggregates of microcycles
- Sub-phases: aggregates of macrocycles, are generally divided into General Preparation, Special Preparation, Pre Competition, Competition, and Transitional.
- Phases: Prepatory, Competitive, Transitional

Notice that, while the terms are a little different, the underlying principles are the same as with Matveyev. Unlike Matveyev, Bompa's book comes in very handy with a number of practical recommendations about setting up the training process. Bompa offers guidelines for the constructing of microcycles and for the periodization of various physical characteristics.

First, Bompa does not feel that each microcycle should be of uniform intensity. In other words, the entire week of training won't be at the same percentage of 1-RM. He recommends setting up microcycles with the following guidelines:

- Begin the microcycle with a low- or medium-intensity day.
- If a microcycle has one peak (i.e. one high-intensity day), that should be towards the middle of the microcycle (see figure 6-6).
- Microcycles with more than one peak should have them evenly distributed throughout the week.
- Microcycles with more than one peak should be surrounded by reduced training loads (see figure 6-7).

Second, Bompa groups exercises by biomotor abilities (strength, endurance, speed, etc.). He feels that different combinations of abilities have different importance for different sports. He does offer recommendations on what abilities should be focused on depending upon where one is in the training process. Figure 6-8 provides a summary of this.

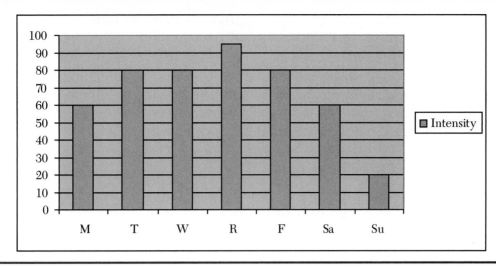

FIGURE 6-6: Microcycle with one peak (Thursday). Note that intensity varies from day to day.

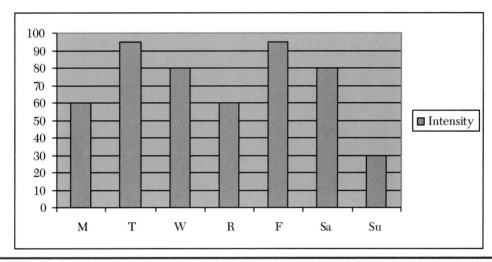

FIGURE 6-7: Microcycle with two peaks (Tuesday and Friday). Notice that reduced intensity days precede both peaks.

	Prepatory		Competition		Transition
	General Prep	Special Prep	Pre Comp	Competition	Transition
Strength	Anatomic Adaptation	Maximum Strength	Conversion: • Power • Musc. Endurance • Both	Maintenance	Compensation
Endurance	Aerobic Endurance		Aerobic Endurance Specific Endurance	Specific Endurance	Aerobic Endurance
Speed	Aerobic and Anaerobic Endruance	Alactic Speed Anaerobic End.	Spec. Speed	Specific Speed Agility Reaction Time Speed Endurance	N/A

FIGURE 6-8: Sample periodization of biomotor abilities.

The recommendations laid out in figure 6-8 give guidelines about what physical qualities should be emphasized depending upon where in the training process one is. They follow the same progressions laid out in Matveyev's plan (i.e. focus on hypertrophy first, then strength, then power) but in a manner that tends to be a little more user-friendly.

Matveyev and Bompa's approaches to periodization are still widely followed in sports conditioning and serve as the foundation for a number of popular books on the subject (see Dick, Freeman, Harre, Kurz, and Nadori for examples). However, these approaches may be difficult to adapt to American athletes due to the different political, educational, and athletic systems that exist in the U.S. As a result, Stone et al. developed a more "American" approach to periodization of training.

Stone and Periodization

Stone, et al's approach to periodization was developed in a 1981 article examining its effects over six weeks with college students enrolled in weight training classes. Stone, et al's original model was developed around four periods. These periods are preparation, transition 1 (transition between preparation and competition), competition, and transition 2 (active rest and recovery). This model has evolved over the years to the point where it is employed in the National Strength and Conditioning Association's *Essentials of Strength Training and Conditioning,* 2nd Edition. Figure 6-9 shows an overview of the current model including volume and intensity guidelines.

As with Matveyev and Bompa's approaches, the intensity is slowly increasing as the athlete progresses through the training year. As intensity increases, volume decreases. This model has an advantage in that it allows for great flexibility in terms of microcycle loading - one may have microcycles of uniform intensity (as in Matveyev) or of varied intensity (as in Bompa).

However, this model does have drawbacks:

- It hasn't really changed much since 1981.
- It is not helpful when it comes to integrating other types of exercise, such as speed or agility training. Clearly there are no guidelines for speed, agility, or endurance training with this approach - this is purely a weight-room approach. Unfortunately, those other types of exercise are very important.

Period	Preparation			Competition		Active Rest
	Off Season	Off Season	Off Season/ Pre Season	In Season	In Season	Off Season
Phase	Hypertrophy	Strength	Strength/ Power	Peaking Öor-	Maintenance	Active Rest
Intensity (% of 1-RM)	Low to moderate, 50-75%	High, 80-90%	High, 75-95%	Very High, >93%	Moderate, 80-85%	Recreational Activities
Volume (sets x reps)	High to moderate, 3-6x10-20	Moderate, 3-5x4-8	Low, 3-5x2-5	Very low, 1-3x1-3	Moderate, 2-3x6-8	

FIGURE 6-9: "American" periodization model overview.

* ■ It ignores the fact that some sports may not need hypertrophy training. Putting a few pounds of extra muscle mass on some types of athletes may make the performance of their sport more difficult. For example, adding ten extra pounds to a high jumper may make it that much more difficult to clear the bar.

■ The in-season volume can be too low for many sports. It can be very difficult to maintain strength, power, and hypertrophy during a long season with one to three sets of one to three repetitions.

The approaches that have been laid out are not without critics. The remainder of this chapter will cover the criticisms of the approaches of periodization that have been described as well as discuss how periodization may be modified with these criticisms in mind.

LIMITATIONS OF PERIODIZATION

Periodization does have one major limitation: it is not for high level athletes. There are several reasons for this:

1. Traditional periodization often does not work with a high-level athlete's calendar. Often the seasons are so long (162 major league baseball games, an almost year-round competitive season for professional track and field athletes, etc.) that one simply cannot maintain fitness throughout the competitive phase. Doing so would mean that one would not be able to improve performance and may actually regress!

2. There is little or no general preparation to special preparation transfer with high level athletes. As I mentioned before, if you have a low fitness level or are relatively untrained, performing almost any exercises will improve your performance. However, the longer you have trained the more difficult this becomes. Unfortunately, someone who has trained for several years needs to focus on developing sports-specific qualities and skills. If an elite athlete is working on GPP then he or she is not developing those sports-specific qualities and skills.

3. It does not adequately address special preparation and competition needs. If a high-level athlete is spending their time working on general preparation, then he or she is not increasing specific fitness and is not working on competition skills. This means the athlete is falling behind their competition. The bulk of an elite athlete's training needs to focus on competition skills and specific fitness (i.e. power).

4. It does not take into account the fact that different athletes require different amounts of time to develop and maintain a peak. Some elite athletes take two months to peak, some take eight. This means that one model (e.g. the periodization model

mentioned above) will not adequately meet the needs of every high level athlete. Keep in mind that periodization calls for a minimum of twelve to twenty-four weeks to get into peak shape. Verkoshansky (1999) feels that many periodization models are arbitrary, not based upon science, and actually interfere with an elite athlete's development.

If periodization does not apply to high-level athletes, then how should their training be modified? Verkoshansky advocates what he calls "block" training, this is also known as "conjugate" training. In block training, one focuses on an aspect of training (strength or technique.) for two to two and a half months. Focusing almost exclusively on this aspect will create a delayed training effect that will last two-and-a-half months to three months, then that aspect could be focused on again. While focusing on that aspect of training, the volume and intensity should be high enough that performance will initially suffer. Outside each block, maintenance work should be done to maintain the previous quality. Verkoshansky feels that strength blocks should always precede technique blocks, this way technique work is done during the delayed training effect of the strength training. Figure 6-10 provides a graphical representation of block training.

Block training is gaining popularity in Western strength and conditioning literature (see Plisk and Stone, 2003 for an excellent review) but it has shortcomings:

- It was developed in 1981 and 1982. Strength, conditioning, and sports have progressed since then.
- It was developed for track and field therefore it may have little or no application outside those sports.
- According to Zatsiorsky (1995), block training leads to a decrease in nontargeted biomotor abilities. In other words, during the technique block strength will suffer.

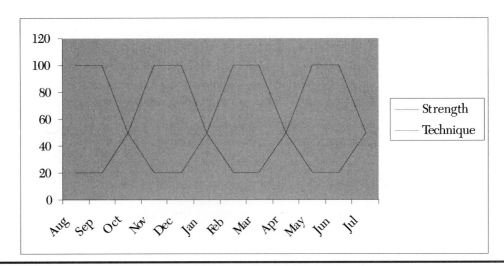

FIGURE 6-10: Sample block training.

So what is one to do with high-level athletes? Rather than rely upon a set-in-stone model, it is probably best to modify them all. The following is a list of modifications that should be made to training programs:

1. elite athletes should perform more special preparation/competition training and less general preparation;
2. different approaches need to be made to volume and intensity than with beginners;
3. exercise selection must be more varied than with beginners; and
4. different training approaches are needed for elite athletes.

First, they should perform more special preparation and competition training and less general preparation. General preparation should make up no more than 20% of an elite athlete's training. The focus of their training should be on strength and power.

Second, there should be different approaches to intensity and volume. Depending upon one's physiological makeup, different people are capable of performing a different volume of work at a prescribed intensity. This is important for an elite-level athlete where every repetition will prove to be critical to success. As a result, a different approach should be made with intensity and volume for elite athletes. A coach should have a range in mind for the athlete (for example: be able to squat four to six repetitions per set with the workout weight). Athletes should be encouraged to do as much as they can, while maintaining good form. In other words, if an athlete is capable of six repetitions at 90% of their 1-RM, with good form, then the athlete should be encouraged to make that happen.

Athletes should also strive to improve their results each time, by either lifting more weight from workout to workout or by performing more repetitions. This is why lifting within a range is a good idea. For example: athlete A squatted 200 kilograms four times during his first squat workout of the month. We want him to squat between four and six repetitions per set. During his second squat workout he should either attempt to squat 200 kilograms five times or attempt 202.5 kilograms four times.

Obviously, one is not going to improve constantly. When one cannot perform more repetitions, or when he or she cannot increase the weight, then the exercises should be changed. For example: if Athlete A cannot squat 200 kilograms five times, or cannot squat 202.5 kilograms four times, then it is time to abandon the squat in favor of another exercise (perhaps a front squat, or bench squat, or pause squat, etc.).

Third, exercise selection needs to be varied. As I described above, exercises should be rotated out when the athlete no longer progresses on them (though they can be re-introduced further down the road). Since elite athletes are by definition good at adapting to exercise, it is important to regularly change the exercises employed to keep them adapting. However, specificity must be observed. This means there must be many exercises that essentially train the same quality that can be integrated into a workout program.

For example, training for lower body strength, the following exercises could be employed (this is not a comprehensive list):

- back squats,
- front squats,
- pause squats,
- bench squats, and
- one-legged squats.

To train the snatch, the following exercises could be employed (this is not a comprehensive list either):

- snatch,
- snatch from blocks, bar above the knee,
- snatch from blocks, bar below the knee,
- snatch from the hang, bar above the knee,
- snatch from the hang, bar at knee height,
- snatch from the hang, bar below the knee,
- snatch with dumbbells,
- one-handed snatch,
- power snatch variations, and
- one-legged snatch.

Fourth, different training approaches are needed for elite athletes. It is acceptable to use a training approach that moves from general preparation to special preparation to competition to transition. However, this should not be used exclusively for reasons that were outlined previously in this chapter. It is also acceptable to use a simultaneous loading approach to training. This means that one works on general preparation, special preparation, and competition exercises at the same time. Bondarchuk (1988a) estimates that using this approach cuts the time to peak in half and allows the athlete to maintain his or her peak much longer (up to 7 months).

Clearly, periodization is a complicated topic that books can (and have) been written on. This chapter has been designed to provide an overview of the basic concepts and most popular approaches as well as inform the reader on where the field seems to be headed and why. The next chapter will present a sample of how to actually periodize a training program integrating some of all of the approaches discussed.

PROGRAM DESIGN

Given all the discussion in previous chapters on training principles and periodization, it should be pretty clear that things can become very complicated quickly. This chapter will help break the program design process into a series of manageable steps that will make the process easier and more realistic than trying to plan out every workout for the entire year ahead of time.

There are a number of steps that should be followed when designing a periodized training plan:

1. determine the sport's annual structure,
2. construct the periods and phases,
3. construct the mesocycles, and
4. construct the microcycles.

DETERMINE THE ANNUAL STRUCTURE

Looking at the calendar to determine the sport's annual structure is important because everything subsequent in the periodization process hinges on this. A few questions to consider:

- When do the competitions fall during the year?
- What days of the week are the competitions on?
- "Is" values vs. "must" values

When Do the Competitions Fall?

Knowing when the competitions occur is important because it will determine the competition period, when the athlete must be peaked, and how many peaks there will be. For example, if (as in college football) the majority of the competitions fall between September and November, then we know that we will need a single peak to the year. On the other hand, if (as in track and field) there are several season (indoor, outdoor, cross-country) then there may be multiple peaks to the year. Understanding when the competitions are allows one to divide the year into periods.

The time around the competitions is the competition period. As we mentioned above, there may be one during a training year or several. Approximately two to four weeks after the competition period should be devoted to rest and recovery if possible (i.e. the transitional period). In some sports this length may not be possible (for example, in track and field there is rarely four weeks between indoors and outdoors). The rest of the time in the training year is the preparation period.

College football will have one peak, which will be from September through November (though it could be longer depending upon bowl games). Football also traditionally has the month of August as a period of heightened intensity, two-a-day workouts, and structured football practices. For this reason, the four weeks of August will be included in the competition period making it sixteen weeks long. The transitional phase will last for five weeks, December through the first week of January. This is being done to take into account the holiday schedule. The rest of the year (second week of January – end of July) will serve as the preparation phase, approximately 29 weeks. Figure 7-1 provides an overview of the structure of the college football training year and its periods.

Period:	Preparation							Competition				Trans
Month:	Jan	Feb	Mar	Apr	May	Jun	Jul	Aug	Sep	Oct	Nov	Dec

FIGURE 7-1: Overview of annual structure and periods for college football.

Track and field is an example of a sport with more than one peak. Track and field has two seasons, the indoor season which runs from January through March (approximately eight weeks) and the outdoor season which runs from March through June or July. December will be included in the competition period as it is also a time of heightened intensity and a change in the means and methods used. Generally there is not a transitional period between the seasons. However, many coaches will train through the first four weeks of the outdoor season, making this a second preparation period. Two to four weeks after outdoors will serve as the transitional period, with the rest of the year being the first preparation period (roughly mid-August through November, fourteen weeks). Figure 7-2 provides an overview of the structure of the college track and field training year and its periods.

Period:	Competition I			Prep II	Competition II			Trans	Preparation I		
Month:	Dec	Jan	Feb	Mar	Apr	May	Jun	July	Aug	Sep	Oct	Nov

FIGURE 7-2: Overview of annual structure and periods for college track and field

Once the periods have been determined, they are then further subdivided into phases. The preparation period is subdivided into the general preparation phase and the special preparation phase. As the general prep phase develops foundational qualities it should make up the bulk of the preparation period. The competition period may be subdivided into pre-competition and competition phases. Pre-competition is designed to be a transition between preparation and competition and should last approximately four weeks.

Looking back at Figure 7-1, we see than January through July is the preparation period for college football (i.e. seven months). To make the bulk of this training general prep, the first four months of this period will be designated as the general preparation phase, with the last three months being special preparation. August will serve as the pre-competition phase, as this is a period with noticeable different training means, methods, and intensities just before the season begins. Figure 7-3 provides an illustration of the college football season.

Period:	Preparation							Competition				Trans
Phase:	General Preparation				Special Preparation			Pre-Comp	Competition			Trans
Month:	Jan	Feb	Mar	Apr	May	Jun	Jul	Aug	Sep	Oct	Nov	Dec

FIGURE 7-3: Overview of periods and phases for college football.

The track and field example, with its two peaks, is a little more complicated. It will also require the breaking of some of the rules that have been mentioned above. First, the bulk of the preparation periods will be spent in special preparation. This is being done due to the nature of the track and field events, with their emphasis on technique, speed, and power. As a result, October and November (eight weeks) will be designated as special preparation, leaving six weeks (mid-August and September) as the general preparation phase during the first preparation period. Second, only the first competition period (December through mid-March) will have a pre-competition phase, which will be the month of December (competitions begin in January). The second preparation period will consist of another special prep phase, this will give the athlete a chance to reduce the intensity somewhat during the four weeks of this phase while focusing on technique, speed, and power shortcomings that were evident during the indoor season. Figure 7-4 provides an illustration of the college track and field season.

Period:	Competition I				Prep II	Competition II			Trans	Preparation I		
Phase:	Pre-C	Comp I			SP II	Competition II			Trans	Gen Prep	Spec Prep I	
Month:	Dec	Jan	Feb	Mar	Apr	May	Jun	July	Aug	Sep	Oct	Nov

FIGURE 7-4: Overview of periods and phases for college track and field.

What Days of the Week are Competitions On?

Knowing what days of the week the competitions occur is also important. If the coach is lucky enough to have the competitions generally occur on the same day of the week (for example, college football and Saturdays) then training can be designed from the very beginning to get the athlete used to being at his or her best on that day of the week. On the other hand, if the sport has competitions on seemingly random days during the week then this must be taken into account as well.

"Is" Values vs. "Must" Values

In addition to the year's structure and the days of competition, two other things should be determined during this phase. This concerns the nature of the evaluations to be used during the training year. In other words, while constructing the year's structure, thought should also be given as to what qualities are important for success in the sport and how those can best be measured. Those measures should then be regularly interspersed throughout the year to help with selection and to help provide feedback about the effectiveness of the training program.

Now that the big picture has been put together, we can begin to get into more detail.

CONSTRUCT PERIODS AND PHASES

Taking the time to make general decisions about the periods and phases will make the planning process much easier down the line. The following steps should be taken to construct periods and phases:

1. make general decisions about the emphasis of each phase, and
2. draw up general guidelines about the training in each phase.

Make General Decisions About the Emphasis of Each Phase

Once the timelines for the training year have been laid out, a coach can begin to make general decisions about what qualities should be emphasized in each period and phase. This is an important step that will make the more detailed planning (mesocycle and microcycle) easier.

For purposes of this book, the following will be the qualities that should be developed in the training plan:

- Hypertrophy
- Strength
- Power
- Speed
- Agility

Hypertrophy refers to two aspects. First, making the muscles larger. Clearly this can be important as we know that strength (and therefore power) can be influenced by the size of the muscles. The other aspect of this is preparing the connective tissue and the skeleton for future intense work. In other words hypertrophy training also has an injury-prevention aspect. This type of training may be multi-joint or single-joint in nature, typically has a moderate number of repetitions with a moderate training intensity.

Strength refers to heavier, multi-joint training. Volume will be lower than with hypertrophy training, intensity will be greater, and there will be longer rest periods. This is important to develop as it is an important aspect of power (i.e. being able to display strength quickly).

Power, in this book, refers to the ability to express strength quickly. There are a number of tools that may be used to train it, everything from Olympic lift variations, to plyometrics, to more traditional exercises performed explosively. The volume will be low, intensity will be moderate to high, and rest periods will allow for complete recovery.

Once the timing of the periods and phases have been determined, one should take some time to make general decisions as to what type of emphasis each of the above qualities should receive in each period and phase. Figure 7-5 provides a sample chart that can be used to help make this decision easier.

Period:	Preparation		Competition		Transition
Phase:	General Prep	Special Prep	Pre Comp	Competition	Transition
Hypertrophy					
Strength					
Power					
Speed					
Agility					

FIGURE 7-5: Sample chart for organizing the emphasis of periods and phases.

Using the chart in Figure 7-5, we may assign a value to each physical quality in each phase. For example; high, medium, and low. A quality with a high emphasis would see the most training sessions, the most intense training, etc. A quality with a medium emphasis would see 2-3 training sessions per week, moderate volume and intensity. A quality with a low emphasis would see 1-2 training sessions per week and the focus would primarily be on maintenance.

Figure 7-6 provides an example of using this chart for college football. The general preparation phase is where the athlete develops his physical base, so the focus is on increasing muscle mass while developing some strength. Power, speed, and agility are all basically maintained during this phase. The special preparation phase continues to see hypertrophy work, while strength becomes the major focus. More power, speed, and agility training is being conducted. In the pre competition phase, weight room activity is decreased due to the rigors of two-a-days. While in season (competition phase), hypertrophy training is maintained, though strength,

Period:	Preparation		Competition		Transition
Phase:	General Prep	Special Prep	Pre Comp	Competition	Transition
Hypertrophy	High	Med/High	Low	Low	Low
Strength	Medium	High	Low/Med	Med/High	Low
Power	Low	Medium	Medium	High	Low
Speed	Low	Medium	High	Medium	Low
Agility	Low	Medium	Medium	High	Low

FIGURE 7-6: Sample chart for organizing the emphasis of periods and phases for college football.

power, speed, and agility are still being aggressively trained. As the transitional phase is meant to be a rest and recovery phase, the emphasis is to maintain each of the physical qualities.

Draw Up General Guidelines About the Training in Each Phase

Now that the content of each phase has been drawn up, it's time to get into a little more detail to help with future planning. Draw up a very rough guide about the types of exercises to be used in each phase, the volume, the intensity, rest/recovery, number of sessions per week, etc. However, at this point remember to keep things general. Figure 7-7 provides a sample of how to do this for the college football example.

Taking the time to think out a chart like in Figure 7-7 will make the program design process easier as it provides training frequency, exercise, volume, and intensity guidelines.

When the broad strokes have been laid out, it's time to begin planning out the individual mesocycles.

CONSTRUCT THE MESOCYCLES

A mistake frequently made by beginning coaches is to attempt to plan out every workout for the entire year ahead of time. It is impractical, unrealistic, and frustrating to do this because the plan must frequently be altered once it meets the athletes. Too many things happen which require altering the plan; athletes don't recover quickly enough, their outside lives interfere, the weather interferes, equipment breaks down, etc. Rather than having to scrap the entire plan, it's better to lay out broad guidelines which provide direction and structure and plan one mesocycle at a time.

To do this, once the broad guidelines have been developed, plan the first mesocycle in detail and the entire phase in principle. Once you are halfway through the first mesocycle, plan the second in detail, etc. Once you are halfway through the phase, plan the next phase in principal, and so forth.

Using the college football example, the first mesocycle (which in our example will last four weeks) is in the general preparation phase. Figure 7-8 summarizes the outline of training in the general preparation phase.

Period:	Preparation		Competition		Transition
Phase:	General Prep	Special Prep	Pre Comp	Competition	Transition
Hypertrophy	4-5x per week Multi-joint and single-joint free weights 3 sets x 8-15 reps 60-80% 1-RM	3-4x per week Multi-joint free weights 3 sets x 8-15 reps 60-80% 1-RM	1-2x per week Multi-joint free weights 3 sets x 12-15 reps 60-70% 1-RM	1-2x per week Multi-joint free weights 3 sets x 12-15 reps 60-70% 1-RM	1-2x per week Single-joint free weights 3 sets 12-20 reps 50-70% 1-RM
Strength	2-3x per week Multi-joint free weights 3 sets x 6-10 reps 70-85% 1-RM	3-4x per week Multi-joint free weights 3 sets x 4-8 reps 75-90% 1-RM	1-3x per week Multi-joint free weights 3 sets x 2-8 reps 75-95% 1-RM	2-4x per week Multi-joint free weights 3-5 sets x 1-6 reps 80-100% 1-RM	
Power	1-2x per week Olympic-style lifts 3 sets x 3-4 reps 60-75% 1-RM	2-3x per week Olympic-style lifts and plyometrics 3-4 sets x 2-4 reps (OL), 3 sets x 10 reps (plyo) 60-80% 1-RM	2-3x per week Olympic-style lifts, plyometrics, and medicine ball 3 sets x 2-4 reps (OL), 3 sets x 10 reps (plyo, MB) 60-80% 1-RM	3-4x per week Olympic-style lifts, plyometrics, medicine balls 3-5 sets x 2-4 reps (OL), 3 sets x 10 reps (plyo, MB) 70-90% 1-RM	Other sports, 2-3x per week
Speed	1-2x per week Falling starts Technique 3-5x10-60 yards	2-3x per week Standing Starts Technique Acceleration Conditioning 2x3-5x10-60 yards	3-5x per week Starts Technique Acceleration Max. velocity Conditioning	2-3x per week Starts Technique Acceleration Max. velocity Conditioning	Other sports, 2-3x per week
Agility	1-2x per week Technique	2-3x per week Technique Combination drills	2-3x per week Technique Combination drills Reactive drills	3-4x per week Combination drills Reactive drills	Other sports, 2-3x per week

FIGURE 7-7: General guidelines for college football training, outline.

Refer back to Figure 7-3, note that the general preparation phase lasts four months. For simplicity, we'll make each month a mesocycle (mesocycles 1-4). Figure 7-9 is an example of planning the general preparation phase in principal.

From Figure 7-9 we can see that the first mesocycle is designed to get the athletes used to organized training again. The phase is designed to be progressively more difficult with volume or intensity increasing on subsequent mesocycles.

Hypertrophy	4-5x per week Multi-joint and single-joint free weights 3 sets x 8-15 reps 60-80% 1-RM
Strength	2-3x per week Multi-joint free weights 3 sets x 6-10 reps 70-85% 1-RM
Power	1-2x per week Olympic-style lifts 3 sets x 3-4 reps 60-75% 1-RM
Speed	1-2x per week Falling starts Technique 3-5x10-60 yards
Agility	1-2x per week Technique

FIGURE 7-8: Summary of training in the general preparation phase.

CONSTRUCT THE MICROCYCLES

Once the phase has been planned in principal, it's time to plan the first mesocycle in detail. The first mesocycle is four weeks long and will therefore have four microcycles (each lasting one week). Training will occur four times per week, with low volume and a lower intensity. We know that there will be

Mesocycle #	Goals	Frequency of Training	Volume	Intensity
1	Begin getting back in shape	4x per week	Low	Averaging 65%
2	Increase frequency of training and volume	5x per week	Moderate	Averaging 65%
3	Maintain frequency and volume, increase intensity	5x per week	Moderate	Averaging 70%
4	Maintain frequency and volume, increase intensity	5x per week	Moderate	Averaging 75-80%

FIGURE 7-9: Planning the general preparation phase in principal.

four training sessions per week. They will be broken up has follows, with the most demanding day on Monday when the athlete is freshest:

- Session 1 (Monday): Power, hypertrophy, strength – total body emphasis
- Session 2 (Tuesday): Speed and agility training
- Session 3 (Thursday): Hypertrophy, strength – lower body emphasis
- Session 4 (Friday): Hypertrophy, strength – upper body emphasis

	Monday	Tuesday	Wednesday	Thursday	Friday	Saturday	Sunday
Hypertrophy	Lying Leg Curls, 3x12 Calf Raises, 3x12 Lat Pulldowns, 3x12 Lateral Raises, 3x12			Lunges, 3x12 Leg Extensions, 3x12 Leg Curls, 3x12 Calf Raises, 3x12	Dips, 3x12 Pull-Ups, 3x12 Dumbbell Shoulder Press, 3x12 Dumbbell Curls, 3x12 Triceps Pushdowns, 3x12		
Strength	Front Squats, 3x8x70% Bench Press, 3x8x70%			Back Squats, 3x8x60% RDL's, 3x8x60%	Incline Press, 3x8x60% Bent Over Barbell Rows, 3x8x60%		
Power	Power Clean, hang, above knee, 3x4x60%						
Speed		Ankling, 2x10 yards Butt kicks, 2x10 yards High knee walks, 2x10 yards Falling Starts, 3x20 yards					
Agility		Shuffle right/left, 2x10 yards Backpedal, 2x10 yards Zig zags, 2x10 yards Cutting 2x5+5 yards					

FIGURE 7-10: Microcycle 1 of the first general preparation mesocycle for college football.

Loading in the mesocycle will take a 3:1 approach, therefore the microcycles will average the following intensities:

Microcycle 1: 60% 1-RM
Microcycle 2: 65% 1-RM
Microcycle 3: 70% 1-RM
Microcycle 4: 65% 1-RM
Figure 7-10 provides a breakdown of the first week in this mesocycle. The rest of the weeks in the mesocycle can be planned out this way.

It's easy to make program design too complicated especially when periodization and annual plans are added to the mix. The steps listed in this chapter have been meant to help simplify this process and to help marry program design to the real world, where plans must frequently be altered due to circumstances beyond the coach's control.

THE BACK SQUAT

The squat is a multi-joint exercise that develops the quadriceps, hamstrings, glutes, calves, erector spinae, and abdominals. It is a foundational exercise that appears in most strength and conditioning programs and is essential for lower body development and strength. Chandler and Stone (1992) report that the squat develops ligament and tendon strength; bone density; the muscles of the hip, knee, and lower back; strength, speed, and power of the leg and hip musculature. The rest of this chapter will discuss how to perform the back squat, how the exercise works, how to spot it, how to perform different variations of the back squat and what benefits they have, and finally it will examine what effects squats have on the knees.

PERFORMING THE BACK SQUAT

To perform the back squat, approach the squat racks and grip the barbell with a pronated grip. Step under the bar so that it rests on the back of your shoulders. Once the bar is on the back of your shoulders, step back from the squat racks. Your feet should be approximately shoulder-width apart. Once your feet are in position, set your back (see chapter three for more information on this).

Once your back is set, squat by pushing your hips back and down. Your hips should start every squatting movement. When your knees start the squatting movement it tends to lift your heels off the floor, transferring much of the stress to your knees. Try to put your stomach between your legs. Keeping your feet flat on the floor, squat down at least until your thighs are parallel to the floor. From the bottom position, extend your hips and knees and stand back up

Depth of the squat will determine both how much weight you can lift and how effective the exercise is. Going to parallel on the squat will involve more muscles, but it will also result in your squatting less weight. On the other hand, if you do not squat down very deeply then you will be able to lift more weight, but the exercise will be less effective.

There are a number of technique errors to watch out for when performing the back squat:

1. *Loss of back set during the squat.* This is easily identified because the shoulders will slump forward and the chest will collapse. This can place a great deal of pressure on the soft tissues of the lower back and could result in injury. Sometimes this is a result of inattention, many beginning lifters simply forget to maintain the proper back position. At other times this will be due to fatigue. If correct technique cannot be maintained then the exercise should be terminated.

2. *Not keeping the feet flat on the floor.* The heels coming up off the ground as the lifter descends into the squat is an error, it should not be acceptable technique. This can be bad for two reasons; first, it can lead to a loss of balance and second, it can result in more stress being placed on the knees. Several things can cause this. First, the lifter may not be using the hips to squat. Frequently beginning lifters will attempt to initiate the squat by pushing the knees forward, this will force heels off the ground as the lifter descends. Second, there may be flexibility issues at the ankle. If this is the case it is a better idea to let the lifter squat as far as he/she can with good technique and gradually increase his/her flexibility over time.

3. *Hips moving faster than the shoulders when standing up.* If the hips move faster than the shoulders during the ascent, then the lifter's upper body will pitch forward as the legs straighten, forcing the lower back to do all the work during the squat. This

can result in excessive stress being placed on the lower back and can also result in a loss of balance. This can be due to bad technique, poor trunk strength, and poor quadriceps strength.

HOW DOES THE BACK SQUAT ACTUALLY WORK?

Recent research has found interesting information on what the back squat does and does not develop. A number of excellent studies by Escamilla, et al., have examined the squat as it is performed by highly skilled athletes (generally squatting double bodyweight or more). In general, Escamilla, et al. (2001) have found a number of interesting things with quadriceps, hamstring, and gastrocnemius activity. With regards to the quadriceps, Escamilla et al. have found that:

- The activity of the quadriceps increases as the lifter descends into the squat.
- Quadriceps activity decreases as the lifter stands up from the squat.
- Quadriceps activity peaks at about 80-90 degrees of knee flexion *and does not increase if the lifter squats lower.* In other words, extremely deep squats will not result in enhanced quadriceps development.
- The vastus lateralis and medialis are 40-50% more active than the rectus femoris in the squat.

With regards to the hamstrings:

- The hamstrings are more active while standing up from the bottom of the squat.
- The hamstrings may fire isometrically throughout the exercise.

With regards to the gastrocnemius:

- Gastrocnemius activity increases as the lifter descends and decreases as the lifter stands up (the gastrocnemius serve to resist the forward movement of the knees during the squat).
- The gastrocnemius may act isometrically throughout the squat.

This data is interesting because in the case of the quadriceps and hamstrings, the recruitment patterns are the opposite of what one would think. One would logically expect the quadriceps to be more active when the knee is extending (i.e. when standing up) and the hamstrings to be more active when the knee is flexing (i.e. when one is descending into the squat). One has to remember that many of these muscles also act on the hip and that appears to take precedence during the squat.

How does the width of the stance affect muscle recruitment? A common myth is that one can selectively recruit various muscles if the foot width is changed or if the toes are turned in or out during the squat. Escamilla, et al. (2001) examined the affects of stance width on muscle recruitment. In general they found that narrow stance squats recruited the gastrocnemius more than wide stance squats, mainly because the knees move forward more during narrow stance squats. Other than that, there is little difference between the stance widths on muscle recruitment!

The angle of the feet also appears to have no affect on muscle recruitment. Escamilla (2001) reports that when the feet are angled at zero degrees (i.e. straight ahead) or angled out at 30 degrees, there is no difference between the two in terms of quadriceps, hamstring, or gastrocnemius muscle recruitment.

While the squat is a highly effective exercise, it can also be a highly dangerous one. Trainees can work up to very heavy weights on this exercise. That, combined with the inherent dangers in the low position (i.e. what if you cannot get up with 400 pounds on your back?) makes it essential that lifters have a spotter when attempting heavy weights and when learning this exercise.

SPOTTING

A spotter should stand behind you and squat down with you during squats. If you get into trouble, the spotter should wrap his or her arms around your chest or under your armpits. Then the spotter should use his or her legs to help you stand up.

When you have more weight than a spotter feels comfortable with, it is advisable to have a spotter on each side of the barbell. This way two people can grab the weight in case of trouble. For extremely heavy weights, it is appropriate to have three spotters, one on each side of the barbell and one behind the lifter.

Having discussed how to perform the back squat and how to spot it, it's time to discuss some of the variations of the back squat. There are many ways this exercise can be performed. This variety is important to keep workouts interesting and effective and it also results in better all-around development.

VARIATIONS OF THE SQUAT

High Bar vs. Low Bar Squats

Two approaches to performing the back squat involve "high bar" squatting and "low bar" squatting. Olympic-style weightlifters and bodybuilders typically use high bar squats whereas powerlifters typically use low bar squats.

High bar squats involve the bar sitting high up on the traps, generally around the level of the lower cervical vertebrae. During this type of squat the torso remains upright, placing the emphasis of the exercise on the quadriceps. This variation results in better development of the quadriceps, but also results in less weight being lifted.

Low bar squats are performed with the bar sitting low on the traps or the rear deltoids. During this type of squat the torso leans forward more, placing the emphasis on the lower back and hips. This variation allows more weight to be lifted, but also potentially puts more stress on the lower back.

Box or Bench Squats

During this exercise, place an adjustable box or bench behind you. Squat down until your glutes touch the box or bench. Pause for a count in the bottom position and then explode up. This variation is designed to help make you more explosive coming out of the low position of the squat. With a pause, there is not possibility of a rebound effect. The height of the box can be adjusted to work on different sticking points of the squat.

This can be an effective exercise to increasing squatting strength and increasing leg strength. However, it can also be very dangerous if performed incorrectly. A number of points are worth remembering:

1. Do not relax in the bottom position. When pausing on the box/bench, make sure to keep your back tight and your shoulders pulled back. Relaxing can cause injury to your lower back and will make the exercise more difficult.

2. Do not bounce off the bench or box. Bouncing will dramatically increase the pressure experienced by your lower back and could injure your vertebrae. Make sure you pause for a full count (one-one thousand) and then explode upward.

Pause Squats

The pause squat is performed just like a high- or low-bar back squat with one exception; pause for a count in the lowest position. In other words, squat down and pause before driving upward. This exercise is meant to increase your strength coming out of the low position of the squat.

A few things to remember about this exercise:

1. Do not relax in the bottom position.
2. Do not rebound out of the low position.

Eccentric Count Squats

These squats are performed with a slow eccentric (i.e. lowering) phase. Set up to perform the squat like you normally would. Take a specified number of seconds to lower yourself down into the bottom position. When you reach the bottom position, immediately drive up as quickly and explosively as possible. This is another exercise designed to increase explosiveness in the squat and leg strength. Generally it is performed with a 10-second eccentric count, in other words the descent takes ten slow seconds.

When it comes to this exercise, remember to stay tight while performing it. This exercise is extremely fatiguing. Make sure to keep your back tight and your shoulders pulled back. Relaxing can cause injury to your lower back and will make the exercise more difficult.

Front Squats

Front squats develop the quadriceps, glutes, and erector spinae muscles. The front squat emphasizes the muscles of the quadriceps and trunk more than the back squat does.

To perform the front squat, start out by gripping the bar with a narrower than shoulder-width grip. Use a pronated grip on the bar. Step under the bar so that the bar is on the front of the shoulders. From here push the elbows upwardly and inwardly. This will rack the bar on the shoulders. Step back from the squat rack. Your feet should be approximately shoulder-width apart. Set your back.

Once you have the bar racked on your shoulders, and once the back is set and your elbows are "high," squat down so that you attempt to place your stomach between your legs. Remember to start the squat with your hips moving back and down. From the bottom position, extend your hips and knees to stand back up.

The front squat can be a very technically demanding exercise. Listed below are a number of pointers to aide in the learning process:

1. With the front squat, you must keep your back set throughout. This is important for keeping the elbows high and the bar racked on the front of the shoulders. If you round your shoulders, you will drop your elbows and lose control of the bar.

2. Keep your feet flat on the floor throughout the squat. Just like with the back squat, if your heels come up off the ground then you will transfer stress to the knees and potentially lose your balance.

3. To prevent the wrist pain for which the front squat is notorious, make sure the barbell is not resting its weight on your wrists. This is usually due to a number of factors:

   ▪ you may be gripping the bar with your hands too wide (i.e. move your hands in closer together);

   ▪ your elbows may be "low" which will force the weight to sit on your wrists; and

   ▪ your back may not be set - which can also cause the weight to sit on your wrists.

You must experiment with this exercise to find what works for you.

There are many variations of the squat exercise; any of which can aid in the strength and development of the lower extremity and trunk. However, a concern has been expressed that the squat exercise could lead to long-term damage of the knee joint. Obviously, if this exercise is bad for the knees then performing it would be counter-productive to conditioning. The remainder of this chapter will examine what effects the squat has on the knee joint.

SQUATS AND THE KNEES

Are squats bad for the knees? This debate has been raging since Karl Klein's study was released in 1961. The rest of this chapter will look at the controversy behind this issue. This chapter will look at three areas:

1. Karl Klein's study,
2. what the research says about squats and the knees, and
3. closed kinetic chain exercises and why they might be good for ACL.

Karl Klein's Study

Karl Klein published a study in 1961 indicating that deep squats were bad for the knees. He used a number of methods to prove this point in his study:

- observing the knee instabilities in 128 competitive weightlifters at the 1959 Pan-American Games, several local colleges, and weightlifting meets held in Texas, and
- observing the knee instabilities in 386 college students who had never done deep squats.

Klein personally conducted knee instability tests on every subject using his own device to measure instability. He compared the weightlifters who routinely performed the deep squat with the students who had never done deep squats. He found the following:

- In the weightlifting group, there was 46% greater medial ligament instability in the right leg and 58% greater medial ligament instability in the left leg than in the no-squatting group.
- In the weightlifting group, there was 67% greater lateral ligament instability in the right leg and 59% greater lateral ligament instability in the left leg than in the no-squatting group.
- In the weightlifting group, there was 16% greater anterior cruciate ligament (ACL) instability in the right leg and 25% greater ACL instability in the left leg than in the no-squatting group.

Klein's recommendations in his study were the following:

1. Deep squats (which he defined as going all the way down, until the hamstrings touch the calves) should be avoided in weight training programs.
2. Deep squats should be replaced with parallel squats (i.e. squat down until your thighs are parallel to the floor), which he called half squats.

Klein's study did not say to avoid doing squats, he merely said they should only be done down to parallel. Needless to say, the results were interpreted as damning for the back squat. Karl Klein's study produced an instant controversy in the strength and conditioning field. While Klein's evidence looks conclusive, there have been problems with duplicating it.

What the Research Says

So are squats bad for the knees? Klein's study would seem to indicate that at least deep squats are. This has been a hotly debated topic in the weight training field and it has been extensively researched. So far, not one study has been able to link deep squats with knee injuries.

Meyers (1971) trained subjects for eight weeks on either full squats (deep squats) or half squats. He found that neither kind of squatting had an affect on knee collateral ligament stretch. This is a significant study because he used Klein's own equipment to conduct the measurements.

Chandler, et al (1989) examined the effects of eight weeks of either full or half squats on the knees. They determined that knee stability was not reduced or increased by eight weeks of either full or half squats. Further, when testing the knees of elite/master level powerlifters and weightlifters, they found that those athletes did not have a decrease of knee stability due to squats.

Chang, et al (1988) found that when compared to non-powerlifters, powerlifters have less range of motion in terms of hip flexion/rotation and knee flexion. In other words, powerlifters are not "looser" than non-powerlifters, in fact they may be tighter.

The three studies quoted above failed to demonstrate that squats were bad for the knees. One (Meyers) even used Klein's own equipment. How could Klein find conclusive evidence about the effects of squats and the knees while no one else is able to repeat it? Terry Todd (1984) has suggested that there may have been some methodological problems with Klein's research.

Current research on the squat and the knees determines a number of interesting things with regards to tibiofemoral compression, ACL tension, PCL tension, and patellofemoral compression.

Tibiofemoral compression refers to the interaction of the femur on the tibia. Too much tibiofemoral compression could damage the articular cartilage of the knee and the menisci. Having said that, it is important because it resists the forward motion (translation) of the tibia relative to the femur. In other words, it is important because it protects the cruciate ligaments of the knee. Escamilla, et al (2001) have found that when compared to narrow-stance squats, wide-stance squats demonstrate greater levels of tibiofemoral compression. They also found that tibiofemoral compression increases as the knees flex and decreases as they extend.

To further support the studies mentioned above, Escamilla, et al. (2001) have not found any ACL tension from performing squats. This is in contrast to the leg extension exercise, where the ACL is loaded as the knee nears full extension.

The posterior cruciate ligament (PCL) is a different matter. PCL tension increases as the knees flex and peaks at maximum knee flexion in the squat. For this reason Escamilla, et al. (2001) recommend avoiding squats at greater than 50-60 degrees of knee flexion if a PCL injury exists.

Patellofemoral compression (or the interaction of the patella on the femur) increases as the knees flex and decreases as they extend. According to Escamilla, et al. (2001) it is somewhat higher in wide-stance squats than in narrow-stance squats. Escamilla, et al. (2001) recommend avoiding squats at greater than 50-60 degrees of knee flexion if a patellofemoral injury exists.

This is not to say that it is impossible for squats to hurt the ligaments of the knees. The next section of this chapter will cover under what conditions squats could be bad for the ligaments of the knees.

When Squats Could Hurt the Knees

The above is not meant to suggest that squats don't have the potential to be bad for the knee ligaments. Several things could result in injuries from performing squats:

1. Bouncing out of the bottom position of the squat, which could increase the shear force experienced by the knees.
2. Letting the knees travel excessively forward during the squat, which could also increase the shear force experienced by the knees. This is usually a result of squatting from the knees instead of the hips.
3. Losing your balance (i.e. feet not flat on the ground), which can cause fluctuations in the amount of force experienced in the joints.

Squats (deep or otherwise) do not appear to be bad for the knees *if they are done properly.* As mentioned in an earlier chapter in this book, correct technique is critical to avoiding injury on squats. Remember, your feet must stay flat on the ground during the entire squat. In addition, remember to use your hips first (i.e. your hips should move back and down during the squat) instead of your knees. This will do two things. First, it will help keep your feet flat on the floor. Second, it will help keep your knees from moving forward excessively.

In fact, squats may be more beneficial to the knees than other exercises such as leg extensions and leg curls. This is due to the fact that squats are a closed kinetic chain exercise.

Closed Kinetic Chain Exercises

A closed kinetic chain exercise is one where your foot meets resistance (i.e. the ground) when you perform the exercise. During an open kinetic chain exercise (like the leg extension) your foot does not meet resistance but is free to move.

Why is this distinction important? It is important because of the nature of the muscles that act on the knee and hip. Your quadriceps act to extend your knee, but they also act to flex your hip (i.e. lift your knee up towards your body). Your hamstrings act to flex your knee, but they also act to extend your hip (i.e. move your leg behind your body). So when you perform a squat, some interesting things happen:

1. During the descent: Your hips and your knees flex to allow you to lower your body. That means that both your quadriceps (hip flexors) and your hamstrings (knee flexors) are contracting to lower your body at the same time.

2. During the ascent: Your hips and knees extend to allow you to raise your body. That means that both your quadriceps (knee extensors) and your hamstrings (hip extensors) are contracting to raise your body at the same time.

This phenomena of both the hamstrings and quadriceps contracting at the same time is called *co-activation.* Why is this important? It is important because co-activation of the hamstrings may reduce the amount of strain experienced by the knee and its ligaments.

When performing an open kinetic chain exercise like the leg extension, only the knee is flexing and extending; the hip is not. That means that there is no co-activation to reduce the load on the knee.

So exercises like leg extensions and leg curls may be worse for the knees than exercises like squats and leg presses!

The back squat is a foundational exercise that develops the lower back and trunk. It has a number of variations that are just as effective at developing the strength and muscles of the lower body. There have been concerns about the long-term safety of this exercise, but those concerns have not been duplicated in the research. The back squat appears to be a necessary, effective, and safe exercise that should be included in most conditioning programs.

Lower Body Exercises

Back squats are not the only exercise that may be used to condition the muscles of the lower extremity. This chapter will describe several other exercises that can be used for this same purpose. This chapter will cover the leg press, the lunge and its variations, leg extensions, variations of the leg curl, and variations of the calf raise.

The first two exercises that will be discussed are closed kinetic chain exercises, the benefits of which were described in chapter eight.

LEG PRESS

The leg press is an exercise that develops the quadriceps, hamstrings, glutes, and calves. It has two advantages over squats; first there is not much technique to the leg press so it is often easier to learn. Second, it does not stress the lower back as much as squats which makes this exercise ideal for people who are not in shape or who have back injuries.

To begin this exercise, lie in the leg press. Make sure that your back is fully supported. Place your feet approximately shoulder-width apart on the platform. Extend your knees and hips. Release the safety catches on the leg press. Once you have released the safety catches, lower the weight until your knees form at least a 90 degree angle. From the bottom position, extend your knees and hips. When you are finished with your set, engage the safety catches so that the weight does not fall on you.

Most leg press machines are built with safety pins to keep the weight from crushing you if you get into trouble. If your leg press doesn't have them, then spotters are necessary on this exercise. Spotters should stand at either end of the machine and should use their entire body to help push the weight.

There are three common errors that are seen on this exercise:

1. Letting your back come off the pad when lowering the weight. This is caused by letting the knees come too far back, when this occurs the hips are lifted up and the lower back leaves the pad. This can place an excessive amount of stress on your lower back.

2. Not keeping your feet flat on the platform. Just like with the back squat, letting the heels come up increases the stress on your knees. Focus on pushing through the middle of the foot to keep this from happening.

3. Letting the knees travel too far forward. In the bottom position, your knees should not travel past your toes. If they do, this indicates that you will need to place your feet higher up on the leg press platform. Letting the knees travel too far forward can place excessive stress on them just like during the back squat.

THE LUNGE

Lunges are performed to develop the quadriceps, hamstrings, and glutes. They also provide a way to develop unilateral strength, mobility, and balance. There are several popular variations of lunges that may be performed to add variety; the ones that this book will cover are forward lunges, walking lunges, reverse lunges, and side lunges.

Forward Lunges

To begin forward lunges, the bar should rest on the back of your shoulders (just like in the back squat). The bar should be gripped with a pronated grip. With the bar on the back of your shoulders, step back from the squat racks. Your feet should be approximately hip-width apart. Set your back. From the starting position, step forward with one foot approximately 30 inches. You want to land on the heel of the lead foot. Flex the lead knee and hip until the thigh is parallel to the floor. The front foot should be flat. The front lower leg should be almost perpendicular to the ground. The ball of the back foot should be in contact with the ground with a slight bend in the back leg. The back foot should be pointed straight ahead. From the bottom position, extend the front knee and hip and take one or two small steps backwards with the front leg until you are back in the starting position. Repeat until the desired number of repetitions have been achieved with the first leg, then switch legs.

Several errors are commonly seen when performing forward lunges:

1. Not stepping forward far enough. If the lifter does not step forward far enough then the front knee will travel forward past the toes. Remember, you want the lower part of that front leg to be perpendicular to the floor. Allowing the knee to travel past the toes could result in excessive stress being placed on the knee joint. If the knee travels out past the toes, this indicates that a larger step needs to be taken.

2. Loss of back set. Just like with the squat and its variations, this can lead to back injuries if you do not keep your back set throughout.

3. Landing on a flat foot. Landing on a flat foot interrupts the natural rhythm of the lift. This sudden braking can lead to knee or back injuries and could result in a loss of control of the barbell. Focus on performing the lunge in a heel-to-toe manner.

Walking Lunges

Walking lunges are very similar to forward lunges except they involve lunging somewhere. Walking lunges start out in the same manner as a forward lunge, except you should be facing an open area. Lunge forward

with one leg. Using your front leg, raise yourself up and bring your ba
forward until your back foot is next to your front. Lunge forward with
opposite leg. Continue alternating until the desired distance or the de
number of repetitions have been covered.

Reverse Lunges

Reverse lunges require more balance than forward or walking lunges. They
also tend to train the hamstrings and glutes more than the other two types of
lunges. The reverse lunge begins just like the forward or walking lunge (i.e.
stand up tall, bar on the back of the shoulders). However, in the reverse
lunge you should take a large step *backwards* and flex the front hip and
knee. You should step back until the front thigh is parallel to the floor and
the front lower leg is perpendicular to the floor. Using the front leg, extend
the knee and hip and bring the back foot forward back to the starting
position. Repeat until the desired number of repetitions have been
performed and then switch legs. Unlike walking lunges, the goal is not to go
anywhere with reverse lunges.

Side Lunges

Side lunges continue to train the glutes, hamstrings, and quadriceps.
However, this exercise also targets the abductors and adductors of the hip.
This exercise has the same starting position as the previous types of lunges
covered in this chapter. To perform a side lunge, take a big step to the left,
leaving the right foot in place. As you step to the left, flex the left knee and
hip so that the left thigh is parallel to the floor and the left shin is
perpendicular to the floor. The right leg should be straight and both feet
should face straight ahead. From this position the right foot can be brought
towards the left or the left can be brought towards the right.

The leg press and lunge develop a variety of lower extremity muscles: the quadriceps, hamstrings, and calves. They are also closed kinetic chain exercises, which means that some co-activation takes place at the knee joint to reduce some of the strain experienced by that joint. The remainder of this chapter will discuss exercises that are "isolation"-type exercises, i.e. they focus on a specific muscle group.

LEG EXTENSIONS

Leg extensions are performed to develop the quadriceps. They are an example of an open kinetic chain exercise. To perform the leg extension, sit in the leg extension machine. Insure that the front of your ankles are against the ankle pads. Extend your knees until your lower leg is parallel to the floor. Lower the weight slowly and repeat.

There are two major errors that are commonly seen with performing leg extensions:

1. Swinging or jerking to get the weight up. This is a single-joint exercise. This means there is no co-activation of the hamstrings to take any of the strain off the knee joint. As a result, swinging or jerking to lift more weight will result in dramatically more strain on the joint and could result in injury.

2. Bouncing the weight. Sometimes trainees will try to lower the weight so quickly that they can get a rebound effect from the weight's bouncing off the other weights in the weight stack. This is not a good idea because of the dramatic fluctuations in the amount of load the knee joint will experience. It is a better idea to lower the weight slowly due to the nature of this exercise (i.e. single-joint).

Leg extensions are meant to develop the quadriceps. They are not the only form of "isolation" exercise for the lower extremity. Leg curls are used to develop the opposing muscle group, the hamstrings.

LEG CURLS

Leg curls are meant to develop the muscles of the hamstrings. These are also open kinetic chain exercises. The two variations of this exercise that we will discuss are lying leg curls and seated leg curls.

Lying Leg Curls

To perform this exercise, lie face down on the leg curl machine. Place your ankles under the padded crossbar with your legs straight. Make sure that your knees are slightly off the bench, this will help alleviate discomfort.

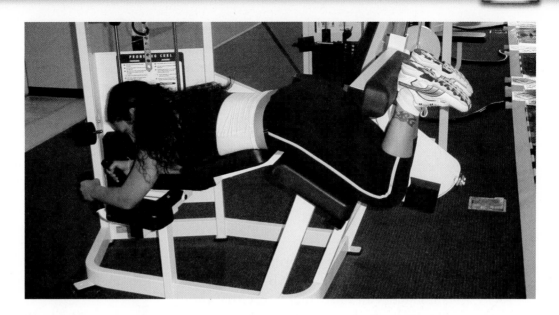

From this position, contract your hamstrings so that the crossbar reaches a position near your hips. Slowly lower the weight and repeat.

A number of errors should be avoided when performing lying leg curls:

1. Do not arch the lower back or raise the hips off the bench. This is done to give the trainee a mechanical advantage when performing the exercise. It should be avoided because it can place unwanted stress on the lower back.

2. Lower the weight under control. Failure to control the weight could result in a pulled muscles or worse.

Seated Leg Curls

To perform this exercise, sit in the leg curl machine. Place your ankles over the padded crossbar with your legs straight. From this position, contract your hamstrings so that the crossbar reaches a position near your hips. Slowly return the weight and repeat.

Once again, make sure to keep control over the weight.

As we have seen leg extensions are used to develop the quadriceps. Leg curls are used to develop the hamstrings. The final muscle group in the lower body to focus on is the calves.

CALF RAISES

Calf raises are used to focus on the gastrocnemius and soleus muscles. There are three variations that we will cover: standing calf raises, leg press calf raises, and seated calf raises.

Standing Calf Raises

This exercise focuses primarily on the gastrocnemius muscles. To perform the standing calf raise, make sure that the shoulder pads are adjusted to approximately shoulder height. This should allow enough range of motion to perform the exercise.

Once the desired height has been selected for the shoulders pads, step onto the machine so that your shoulders are underneath the pads. Place both feet on the block and straighten your legs. Keeping your trunk and your legs straight, position your feet so that the balls of your feet are in contact with the block but your heels are not. Your heels should be pointed towards the floor and your calves should be fully stretched out.

From the starting position, using only your calf muscles, rise up onto your toes as high as you can. Lower yourself slowly and repeat.

Note that this exercise may also be done with a barbell on the back of your shoulders.

Two common errors are made with standing calf raises:

1. Failure to get a good stretch at the bottom of the exercise. The heels should be pointing as far down as possible. Doing this allows one to work the muscle through its entire range of motion; however it also results in less weight being lifted.

2. Failure to go up onto the toes at the top of the exercise. Many lifters will perform a mid-range calf raise (not too high up, not too low) which allows a maximum amount of weight to be lifted. This should be avoided as the calf muscles should be taken through a full range of motion during training.

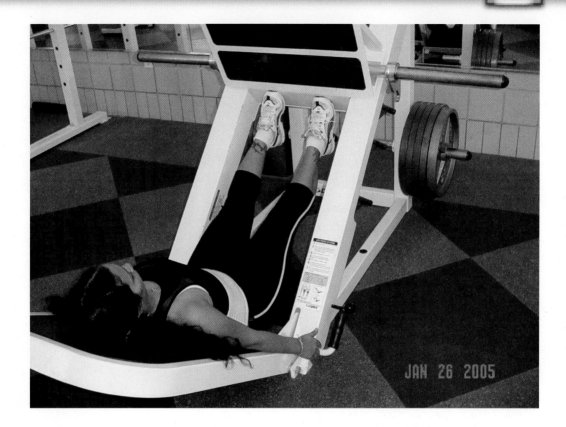

JAN 26 2005

Leg Press Calf Raises

Like the standing calf raise, this exercise focuses more on the gastrocnemius. Unlike the standing calf raise, this exercise does not directly load the lumbar spine. For that reason people with back pain will prefer this variation.

For this exercise, sit in the leg press. Keep the safety catches engaged at all times during this exercise. This will keep you from being crushed if your feet slip off the leg press.

Place your feet on the bottom of the leg press platform so that the balls of your feet are in contact with it. Extend your legs so that the leg press is no longer resting on the supports. From this position, relax your calf muscles and stretch out your calves (this should move the platform closer to you). From the start position, *using your calves,* attempt to point your toes. Try to move the platform as far away from you as possible, using your calves.

Two common errors are made with leg press calf raises:

1. Failure to get a good stretch at the bottom of the exercise.
2. Failure to go up onto the toes at the top of the exercise.

Seated Calf Raises

The seated calf raise is an exercise that focuses more on the soleus than on the gastrocnemius. To perform the seated calf raise, sit on the calf raise machine. Place your legs under the thigh pads, so that the pads sit on your thighs just above your knees. Make sure that the balls of your feet are on the block. Release the safety catch and stretch your calves. Keeping the balls of your feet on the block, lower your heels and attempt to point them towards the floor. From that position, using only your calf muscles, rise up onto your toes as high as possible. Lower slowly and repeat.

Two common errors are made with seated calf raises:

1. Failure to get a good stretch at the bottom of the exercise.
2. Failure to go up onto the toes at the top of the exercise.

THE BENCH PRESS

The bench press is one of the most widely recognized upper body exercises. It is used to develop the pectoralis major, triceps brachii, and anterior deltoids. It is widely employed in conditioning programs and is a test that is frequently used in athletic programs. It aids a number of sports including throwing and football. This chapter will discuss how to perform the bench press, how to spot it, and what variations of this exercise may be performed.

PERFORMING THE BENCH PRESS

To perform the bench press, lie on the bench and position yourself so that your eyes are directly under the barbell. This is important because when you position yourself so that your shoulders are directly under the bar, you will tend to push the barbell into the uprights. On the other hand, sitting too far up on the bench (i.e. with the barbell behind the head) makes spotting difficult. Make sure that your head, shoulders, and buttocks are in contact with the bench and that your feet are flat on the floor. Grip the barbell with a pronated grip that is wider than shoulder-width.

Some individuals will perform the bench press with their feet on the bench. By and large this should be discouraged as it makes controlling the barbell difficult (loss of balance is very easy in this position). This variation would be beneficial to an individual with a lower back injury, however, as the feet being on the bench would help to keep the lower back flat relieving some of the pain that the bench press could cause.

The barbell should be taken from the racks and held with the arms fully extended. The bar should be held in a position that is directly over the middle of your sternum (i.e. around the second rib). From the starting position, lower the barbell until it touches your chest at around the nipple level. Do not bounce the bar off your chest. Once the bar has touched your chest, extend your arms to press the barbell back to the starting position, i.e. the barbell should be pressed at an arc so that it is back over the second rib. The barbell should be pressed until your elbows lock out.

Several errors are commonly made with the bench press:

1. Bouncing the bar off the chest, This allows for a rebound off the chest and does allow for more weight to be lifted. This is also very dangerous and can result in broken ribs. Ciocca, Jr. (2000) relates the case report of a 27-year old man who suffered a collapsed lung from bouncing the barbell off his chest (he fractured ribs which punctured the lung) during the bench press.

2. Not keeping the feet flat on the floor. If your feet leave the floor while the barbell is positioned above the chest, this can result in an unstable lifting position and can cause you to lose your balance possibly resulting in injury.

3. Failure to keep the buttocks on the bench. When attempting too much weight, many trainees will resort to extending their legs and lifting their hips off the bench to help them perform the lift. Lifting the hips off the bench while performing the bench press can cause injury to the lower back.

Correct technique is important for performance on the bench press. Due to the nature of the exercise (i.e. one in which the barbell is positioned over the face and neck of the lifter), proper spotting is also important.

SPOTTING THE BENCH PRESS

Spotting is very important on the bench press. If you are tired enough or if there is enough weight on the bar, then the barbell could get stuck on your chest during this exercise pinning you to the bench. Also, if you are tired enough, you could lose control of the bar and set it down on your neck, which could be life threatening.

For the bench press, a spotter should stand behind the head of the bench. When the lifter needs help, the spotter should grip the bar using a mixed grip, with the spotter's hands inside the lifter's. The spotter should use his or her legs to lift the barbell off the lifter.

Now that we've covered fundamental technique and safety, realize that there are a number of variations of the bench press that can be used in training. These may be used to develop specific muscles or to strengthen specific phases of the bench press.

VARIATIONS OF THE BENCH PRESS

Close Grip Bench press vs. Wide Grip Bench Press

Performing the bench press with a narrower grip will result in the sternal portion of the pectoralis major being taxed more heavily along with the triceps brachii. The close grip bench press is an exercise that is typically used for tricep and inner chest development. Because of the narrower grip, the path the barbell must travel will be lengthened resulting in less weight being lifted. To perform this exercise, grip the barbell with a grip-width that is narrower than shoulder-width apart. As you lower the barbell to your chest, make sure to keep your elbows in towards your body. Ideally your elbows should brush against your body. This makes control of the barbell easier during the exercise.

The most common error seen with the close grip bench press is to have the hands too close together. This makes control of the barbell very difficult, in fact if your hands are too close together you will not be able to touch your chest with the barbell. Keeping the hands too close together also stresses the wrists.

Performing the bench press with a wider grip will result in the clavicular portion of the pectoralis major being taxed more heavily. This form of the bench press shortens the path of the barbell, allowing more weight to be lifted. To perform this exercise, grip the barbell so that your hands are wider than shoulder-width. Keep your elbows out as you lower the bar.

Towel Bench Press

The towel bench press is designed to limit the range of motion. This is an exercise that is used with individuals who have a shoulder injury. It is also an effective exercise for strengthening the triceps brachii and the lockout phase of the bench press. To perform the towel bench press, get a large bath towel. Roll it up and place it on your chest. From here, perform the bench press normally. Realize that the towel will limit how far down the barbell will go, thus your triceps will be the major muscle group trained on this exercise.

One error to be aware of, having the towel on your chest does not mean that it is safe to bounce the barbell off your chest! Just because you have some cushioning between you and the barbell does not make it any safer...

Reverse Grip Bench Press

The reverse grip bench press is designed to develop the triceps brachii, which will help in training the lock-out phase of the bench press. This exercise is performed exactly like the regular bench press with one exception, your hands should be suppinated. Other than that, the exercise should resemble the bench press. Grip the barbell in the same place; lie on the bench the same way; bring the barbell down to the same point on your chest; etc.

One note of caution about this exercise, try to avoid hyperextending your wrists during the execution of the reverse grip bench press. This exercise can cause pain to the wrists if they are allowed to hyperextend. Try to keep your wrists straight, even though this will require concentration at first.

Floor Press

The floor press is designed to limit the range of motion. This is an exercise that could be used with individuals who have a shoulder injury. It is also an effective exercise for strengthening the triceps brachii and the lockout phase of the bench press.

The floor press is best performed in a cage. To perform this exercise, lie on the floor. The pins in the cage should be adjusted so that a lifter may lie on the floor while being able to reach up and grab the barbell with a slight bend in their arms.

Lie on the floor under the barbell. Your eyes should be directly in line with the barbell (just like in the bench press). This exercise is performed exactly like the bench press with one exception, the floor will limit how far down you can lower the barbell. Once the back of your arms contact the floor, press the barbell upwards explosively. You should maintain the same bar path that you do during the bench press (i.e. do not get in any bad habits here!).

With this exercise, do not bounce your arms off the floor. Lower the bar, touch the floor with the back of your arms, then explode up.

Dumbbell Bench Press

This variation forces one to develop better balance and coordination due to the demands that two dumbbells place on the body. It also allows for a better stretch on the pectoralis muscles due to the fact that the dumbbells may be lowered more than the barbell.

Begin this exercise with a dumbbell in each hand. Sit on the edge of a bench and make sure the dumbbells are sitting on your thighs. Starting with the dumbbells in this position will make it easier to get the dumbbells to your chest in the next step. From the seated position, lay back on the bench and bring the dumbbells to your chest (all at the same time). If this is done correctly, then the dumbbells should be at the edge of your chest, near your armpits. Your elbows should be underneath the dumbbells.

From the start position, press the dumbbells up until your arms are extended. As your arms extend, move the dumbbells together slightly. Do not let them touch at the top. Lower the dumbbells slowly and repeat.

The bench press is one of the fundamental exercises in upper body conditioning. Performing it correctly is key to realizing the benefits it can provide and is important for safety. There are a number of variations that are possible that may assist the bench press, train portions of the lift, or just hit the upper body in a different way. These variations can also make a workout more interesting by changing things up.

UPPER BODY: "PUSHING" EXERCISES

The bench press and its variations are not the only exercises that may be performed to train the muscles of the chest, shoulders, and the back of the arm. This chapter will describe a number of exercises that are good to include in a strength and conditioning program to provide variety to training for those muscles. These exercises allow one to attack the chest, shoulders, and triceps from different angles resulting in more complete development.

PRESSES

Presses, or "pushing" exercises, should form the backbone of training for the chest, shoulders, and triceps. These multi-joint exercises may be performed with barbells, dumbbells, there are machine variations, and some may even be performed standing or seated. The combination allows for a great deal of variety and allows the trainee to target his/her muscles from a variety of different angles. The following exercises will be covered:

- incline press,
- decline press,
- dips,
- behind the neck press,
- military press, and
- dumbbell shoulder press.

Each exercise will be discussed in terms of technique, variations, and spotting.

Incline Press

The incline press develops the pectoralis major, anterior deltoid, and triceps brachii. Unlike the bench press, this exercise emphasizes the superior (clavicular) portion of the pectoralis major. Due to the angle at which this exercise is performed, it will be more difficult than the bench press, so you will lift less weight on this exercise. Depending on the angle of the bench, different muscles may be emphasized in this exercise and this may affect how much weight you can use. A steeper angle will emphasize the anterior deltoids more and the pectoralis major less. As the angle gets closer to a completely flat bench, the pectoralis muscle will become more involved in the exercise, allowing more weight to be lifted.

To perform this exercise, lie flat on the bench with your feet flat on the floor and your shoulder blades and buttocks in contact with the bench. Some benches are made with a platform for your feet. If that is the case, then attempt to keep your feet flat on the platform.

Position yourself on the bench so that your eyes are ahead of the barbell. Grip the barbell with the same grip you used on the bench press. Take the bar from the racks so that you begin the exercise with your arms fully extended. The barbell should be positioned over your clavicles/upper chest.

From the starting position, lower the barbell until it touches your chest just below your clavicles. Do not bounce the barbell off your chest. Once the barbell has touched your chest, press the barbell back to the starting position (i.e. over the clavicles/upper chest).

There are several common errors that are made during the incline press. First, bouncing the barbell off the chest should be avoided. Second, the feet need to be kept flat on the floor or platform. Third, care should be taken to avoid placing the barbell on either the collarbones or the neck as this can be both painful and interfere with breathing. Fourth, if the barbell is placed too low on the chest, this can make the bar much more difficult to control.

The incline press is another exercise where the barbell could get stuck on you if you are too fatigued or if there is too much weight on the bar. As a result, a spotter is necessary for this exercise. A spotter should stand behind the incline bench. Some incline benches have platforms for the spotter to stand on. When you need help, the spotter should grip the bar with a mixed grip and use his or her legs to help lift the bar.

The incline press may also be performed with dumbbells. Like with the dumbbell bench press, this variation forces you to develop better balance and coordination due to the demands that two dumbbells place on the body. It also allows for a better stretch on the pectoralis muscles due to the fact that the dumbbells may be lowered further than the barbell.

Begin this exercise with a dumbbell in each hand. Sit on the incline bench and make sure the dumbbells are sitting on your thighs. From the seated position, lay back on the bench and bring the dumbbells to your chest. If this is done correctly, then the dumbbells should be resting in the groove between your shoulders and chest. Your elbows should be underneath the dumbbells.

From the start position, press the dumbbells up until your arms are extended. As your arms extend, move the dumbbells together slightly. Do not let them touch at the top. Lower the dumbbells slowly and repeat. Avoid arching your back or lifting your buttocks off the bench while performing the incline press with dumbbells.

Decline Press

The decline press is performed on a bench that will allow your head to be lower than your feet. Performing the exercise in this manner will develop the pectoralis major, anterior deltoids, and triceps brachii. However, due to the angle, this exercise will have a similar difficulty level to the bench press; therefore similar weights may often be used.

To perform this exercise, lie flat on the bench with your feet secured under the restraints and your shoulder blades and buttocks in contact with the bench. Due to the design of the decline benches, you may not be able to position yourself so that your eyes are under the barbell. If the bench places you in an unfavorable position you will need assistance lifting the barbell off the racks. Grip the barbell with the same grip you use on the bench press. Take the bar from the racks so that you begin the exercise with your arms fully extended. The barbell should be positioned over the middle of your sternum.

From the starting position, lower the barbell until it touches the lower portion of your chest (at nipple line or slightly lower). Once the barbell touches your chest, press it up. Press the barbell up at a slight angle so that it ends up positioned over the middle of your sternum. Do not bounce the barbell off your chest.

The decline press is another exercise where the barbell can get stuck on you if you are too fatigued or if there is too much weight on the bar. As a result, a spotter is necessary for this exercise. The spotter should stand behind the decline bench. When you need help, the spotter should grip the bar with a mixed grip and use his or her legs to help lift the bar.

Like the bench press and incline press, the decline press may also be performed with dumbbells. Begin this exercise with a dumbbell in each hand. Sit on the decline bench with your feet secured making sure the dumbbells are sitting on your thighs. Lay back on the bench and bring the dumbbells to your chest. If this is done correctly, then the dumbbells should be resting at the side of your chest near your armpits (just like in the dumbbell bench press). Your elbows should be underneath the dumbbells.

From the starting position, press the dumbbells up until your arms are extended. As your arms extend, move the dumbbells together slightly. Do not let them touch at the top. Lower the dumbbells slowly and repeat.

Dips

Unlike incline and decline presses, dips do not use a barbell or dumbbell. They require parallel bars and body weight for resistance. As one progresses added resistance may be necessary.

Dips develop the pectoralis major, anterior deltoids, and triceps brachii. The muscles that are primarily emphasized will be determined by how this exercise is performed.

To perform this exercise, grip the parallel bars with a shoulder-width grip. Extend your arms until they are locked out and supporting your weight. Bend your knees slightly and cross your ankles, this is to keep your feet from touching the floor. From the starting position, lower yourself slowly by flexing your elbows. Lower yourself until your upper arms are at least parallel to the floor. From the bottom position, extend your arms until they are locked out again.

 Body lean will affect the muscles that are primarily involved in this exercise. When leaning forward, the pectoralis major is more involved in this exercise. When the torso is more upright, the triceps are emphasized more.

 A number of things should be kept in mind while performing this exercise. First, this exercise should be performed slowly, trying to "bounce" out of the bottom position is extremely dangerous. Second, one should avoid swinging when performing this exercise. This is a frequent problem with beginners and can result in the exercise becoming much more difficult. After assuming the starting position, make sure to steady yourself before executing the exercise. Third, trainees will frequently fail to go down far enough. This results in failing to recruit the pectoralis muscles. Finally, failing to lock out the elbows at the top of the movement will result in the triceps not being completely activated during this exercise.

 During dips, spotting is useful in helping you perform extra repetitions. A spotter should stand behind you on this exercise. Your ankles should be crossed behind you. The spotter will put one forearm under your ankles. The other forearm will be placed just below the knees. From here the spotter should use his or her legs to help drive you up.

What if you cannot perform dips? After all, this is one of those exercises that requires a baseline level of strength and muscle mass to perform. One option is to use an assisted-dip machine. This is a machine that provides assistance when performing the exercise, the more weight that is used the easier the exercise is performed (i.e. fifty pounds represents fifty pounds of assistance). Realize that this approach tends to be a crutch and very few people are actually able to graduate from performing the assisted dip and the unassisted dip. A more effective approach is to perform the following:

1. Perform the presses outlined in chapters ten and eleven to build up the muscle mass/strength necessary to help perform dips.

2. At the same time as #1 above, perform the following progressive exercises to work on strength and technique:

   ▪ Partial dips, feet on floor: For this exercise you need a bench. Sit on the bench, place your hands on either side of your hips. Walk your feet forward until your legs are straight and your hips are off the bench, if this is done correctly then your upper body will be supporting your weight. Keeping your legs straight, flex your elbows and lower yourself until your upper arms are parallel to the floor. As you lower yourself, make sure to keep your elbows pointed to the rear and keep your arms against your sides. Once you have reached the bottom position, extend your arms until your elbows are locked out.

   ▪ Between bench dips: This exercise is performed exactly like the partial dips, only your feet will be on a bench in front of you. Make sure that the bench is far enough away so that your hips are unsupported and your legs are straight.

   ▪ Eccentric-only dips: This exercise helps to further develop strength and refines technique. Approach the parallel bars. Either jump up or have a partner lift you up until you are supporting your bodyweight with your upper body. The starting position should be the same as in the regular dip exercise. From this position, slowly lower yourself until your upper arms are parallel to the floor. Take as long as you can to lower yourself down, fight! Remember to keep your arms at your sides throughout. Once you have reached the bottom position, jump back up (or be lifted back up) and repeat. While difficult, this is an extremely effective variation.

Behind the Neck Press

The behind the neck press develops primarily the anterior deltoids and the triceps brachii with some assistance from the medial deltoids. This exercise also teaches an important lesson; how to balance a weight overhead.

This exercise is performed standing up. To perform this exercise, the barbell should be behind your head, resting on the shoulders. You should grip the barbell with a pronated grip that is slightly wider than shoulder-width. Step away from the squat rack. Your feet should be approximately hip-width apart and your elbows should be under the bar. Set your back. From the starting position, press the barbell straight up until your arms are fully extended. To aid with balance, the barbell should be directly over your hips.

With this exercise, it is very important to keep your back set. Avoid leaning backwards while the weight is overhead as this can cause injury to your lower back. Make sure to keep the bar in line with your hips while pressing it overhead. This will aid with balance. Letting it move too far forward or too far backward will make control difficult and could set you up for a shoulder or back injury.

Spotters are necessary on this exercise. They should have two functions; first, to let you know when the barbell is not over your hips and second, to assist you in performing more repetitions. Because this is a standing exercise and the bar is being put overhead, a spotter may not be able to reach the barbell. As a result, a spotter should grasp your elbows and apply force there to help with the lift.

This exercise may also be performed in a seated position. To perform this variation, sit on a bench with the barbell resting on the back of your shoulders. You may have your back supported (which will make the exercise easier) or unsupported. Regardless, you should make sure to set your back when performing this exercise in order to protect your lower back. Make sure that your elbows begin the exercise directly under the barbell. From the starting position, press the barbell straight up. Just like with the standing variation, make sure to keep the barbell in line with your hips. The seated variations will be a little easier than the standing because you do not have to worry about keeping the weight perfectly balanced.

Caution should be taken with this exercise. This exercise may aggravate shoulder injuries and should be avoided by people who are injured or predisposed to shoulder problems.

Military Press

The military press develops the deltoid muscles and the triceps brachii. It also teaches one to balance with a barbell overhead. It also is one of the lead-up exercises for teaching the jerk (see chapter fourteen for more information on the jerk).

This exercise is also performed while standing. In the military press, the bar starts on the front of the shoulders. You should take a pronated, shoulder-width grip on the bar. Step away from the squat racks. Your feet should be approximately hip-width apart. Set your back. From the starting position, press the bar up and slightly behind the head. The bar should be placed over your center of gravity for balance. It is important that the bar be placed in line with the hips while performing this exercise.

There are a number of common errors to avoid when performing the military press. First, you may lose your back set. This is potentially dangerous to your lower back and will negatively affect your ability to balance the barbell overhead. Second, you may lose your balance with the weight overhead. This results from not keeping the bar over your center of gravity (i.e. over the hips). Remember, the barbell is pressed up and slightly behind your head. Make a point to try to get the bar over your hips Because the lift is started in front of the lifter, a spotter isn't recommended for helping perform this exercise. However, a spotter will be useful in giving you feedback about whether the bar is being placed over your hips.

Like the behind the neck press, this exercise may also be performed sitting down. Once again, it may be done with the back supported or unsupported. To perform this exercise sitting down, begin sitting on a bench with the barbell on the front of your shoulders. Make sure to set your back. From this position press the barbell up and slightly behind your head. Keep the bar over your hips for balance. Lower the barbell under control and repeat. This exercise will be easier in the seated position. This is because balance will not be as much of a limiting factor as when this is performed standing.

bbell Shoulder Press

The dumbbell shoulder press develops the deltoids and triceps brachii. Because it uses dumbbells, it forces you to develop balance and coordination between your right and left sides.

To perform this exercise, stand up with the dumbbells touching the lateral aspect of each shoulder. Grip the dumbbells with a pronated grip. Make sure that your elbows are under the dumbbells. Set your back. From this position press the dumbbells straight up and slightly together. Do not let them touch at the top of the exercise.

When performing this exercise, make sure that you keep your back set and avoid leaning backwards as these mistakes could injure your lower back.

As this is an overhead lift that requires balance and coordination, a spotter is recommended. To spot this exercise, a spotter should stand behind you. When you have trouble pressing the dumbbells, they should place their hands under your elbows and assist by pushing up.

This exercise may also be performed sitting down. As with the first two exercises in this chapter, your back may be supported or unsupported. To perform the dumbbell shoulder press sitting down, sit with the dumbbells touching the lateral aspect of each shoulder. Keep your elbows under the dumbbells. Set your back. Press the dumbbells straight up and slightly together. Lower and repeat. Make sure to keep your back set throughout.

The exercises that have been described to this point are all multi-joint exercises and should form the backbone of a strength and conditioning program for the upper body. The remainder of this chapter will discuss single-joint or isolation exercises that are great for supplementing a strength and conditioning program.

ASSISTANCE EXERCISES

This chapter will cover the following assistance exercises to train the muscles of the chest, shoulders, and triceps; dumbbell flies, lateral raises, rear deltoid raises, triceps pushdowns, and triceps extensions.

Dumbbell Flies

Unlike the other exercises that have been discussed in this chapter, flies are meant to isolate the pectoralis muscles. While other muscles will be involved somewhat, they will not be involved to the same extent that they are during presses and dips.

To perform dumbbell flies, lie on a bench with a dumbbell in each hand. Make sure that your head, shoulders, and buttocks are in contact with the bench. Your feet should be flat on the floor. With a neutral grip, press both dumbbells until the arms are fully extended. The dumbbells should be positioned over your chest. From the starting position, flex your elbows slightly. The elbows should remain in this position throughout the exercise. Slowly lower the dumbbells to your sides. The dumbbells should not be lowered past the level of your chest. Lowering the dumbbells too far can result in damage to the shoulder joint. Once the dumbbells have been lowered, reverse direction and return to the starting position.

With this exercise spotting is not so much for injury prevention as it is for performance enhancement. Here, spotting is used to help you crank out a few extra repetitions. With dumbbell exercises, the spotter should grasp your wrists or forearms and apply force there to help you complete the movement.

Dumbbell flies may be performed on a flat bench like the photos in this chapter have illustrated. They may also be performed on an incline bench or on a decline bench.

Standing Side Lateral Raises

These are designed to stress the medial deltoids. To perform this exercise, stand up with a dumbbell in each hand. You should use a neutral grip. Bend your elbows slightly during this exercise. From this position, using only your shoulders, raise your arms to the sides until they are parallel to the floor. It's generally not a good idea to raise the

arms above the parallel position, doing so increases your risk of shoulder impingement. Lower the dumbbells under control and repeat.

    With this exercise, it is important to keep a slight bend in your arms throughout. Also remember to avoid swinging with your body to lift the dumbbells. Using your entire body to perform the exercise defeats its purpose.

    Note that this exercise can also be performed sitting down.

Bent Over Lateral Raises

This exercise is designed to stress the posterior deltoids, rhomboids, and trapezius. To perform this exercise, stand up with a dumbbell in each hand. Your feet should be approximately shoulder-width apart. From this position, set your back. Push your hips back and bend your knees slightly. Your torso should be 10 to 30 degrees above horizontal. Your arms should hang straight down with the dumbbells directly below your shoulders and a neutral grip. There should be a slight bend in your arms. Point your elbows to the sides. From this position, keeping your torso stationary, raise your arms laterally until they are parallel to the floor. Make sure to keep your elbows slightly bent.

It is important to keep your back set throughout this exercise. Remember to avoid swinging with your entire body, let your shoulders do the work here.

Triceps Pushdowns

Many of the exercises we have previously discussed (i.e. presses) develop the triceps muscles to an extent but do not isolate it. Pushdowns are an exercise that may be used to isolate that muscle group.

To perform the pushdown, you should be standing up in front of the pushdown machine. Grasp the handles with a pronated grip. Bring the bar down so that you begin the exercise with your elbows flexed and pulled tight against your body. From this position, keeping your elbows against your side, use your triceps to push the bar down towards your thighs.

When performing pushdowns, avoid leaning too far forward over the bar. Doing this will give you too much leverage and make the exercise too easy. Make sure to keep your elbows against your body throughout, letting your elbows flare out will take some of the emphasis off your triceps.

Triceps Extensions

Triceps extensions are another exercise that will focus on the triceps muscles. This chapter will focus on the following variations of extensions:

1. lying triceps extensions,
2. seated triceps extensions, and
3. standing triceps extensions.

To perform lying triceps extensions, grasp a barbell and lie down on a bench. Your hands should be pronated and approximately 6-12 inches apart. Extend your arms so that the bar is over your chest. Without moving your upper arms, lower the bar towards your forehead. Do not bounce the bar off your forehead! From that position, using your triceps, raise the weight back to the starting position. Like with pushdowns, avoid letting your elbows flare out during this exercise.

To perform seated triceps extensions, sit down on a bench. a good idea to have something supporting your back during this exercise. Grasp the bar with a pronated grip. You should use the same grip-width that you use on the lying triceps extension. Your arms should be extended over your head. Without moving your upper arms, lower the bar behind your head. From that position, using your triceps, raise the weight back to the starting position. Remember, do not let your elbows flare out.

To perform the standing triceps extension, stand up with the barbell in your hands. Use a pronated grip on the bar. You should have the same grip-width that you use on the lying triceps extension. Your arms should be fully extended over your head. Without moving your upper arms, lower the bar behind your head. From that position, using your triceps, raise the weight back to the starting position. Remember to keep your elbows pulled in while performing this exercise. Do not let them flare out.

Upper Body: "Pulling" Exercises

The exercises that have been described in chapters ten and eleven address movements that (for the most part) train pushing muscles. There is little development of muscles involved in pulling (i.e. upper back and biceps). This chapter will describe pulling exercises that attack those muscles. It will be divided into pulling exercises and assistance exercises. Technique, variations, and (when appropriate) spotting will be covered for each.

PULLING EXERCISES

These exercises represent multi-joint exercises for the muscles of the upper back, shoulder, and biceps. Even though the muscles of the upper back are difficult to see in the mirror, they should not be avoided. These multi-joint exercises should form the foundation of a strength and conditioning program for this part of the body. The following pulling exercises will be covered in this chapter.:

- pull-ups,
- pull-downs,
- rows,
- shoulder shrugs, and
- upright rows.

Pull-Ups

Pull-ups train the latissimus dorsi, rhomboids and biceps. They are an excellent upper body conditioning exercise because they require enough strength in the muscles of the upper back and biceps to enable you to pull your weight up from a dead hang. There are several variations of the pull up that this chapter will cover:

1. wide grip, behind the head;
2. wide grip, to the front; and
3. close grip, to the front.

Of the three variations that will be covered, performing pull-ups with a wide grip and pulling yourself up until the pull-up bar is behind your head will probably be the most difficult. This exercise primarily relies upon the muscles of the upper back (lats and rhomboids) with some assistance from the biceps. To perform this exercise, grasp the bar with a wide, pronated grip.

This exercise begins from a dead hang, i.e. the exercise begins when the feet are no longer in contact with the ground and your arms are fully extended. Without swinging, pull yourself up until the back of your neck touches the bar. Lower yourself until your arms are fully extended and repeat for the desired number of repetitions. When performing this exercise, concentrate on trying to pull your shoulder blades together as you pull yourself up, this will help to focus you on training your upper back muscles. It is important that you try to avoid swinging as this will make the exercise more difficult.

While this is a popular variation of the pull-up, care should be taken when using this exercise. Individuals that are predisposed to shoulder problems should probably avoid performing this type of pull-up.

Of the three variations that will be covered, performing the pull-ups with a wide grip and pulling yourself up until the bar is in front of you will be the in-between version in terms of difficulty. Not only does it rely upon the muscles of the upper back, but it will also recruit the pectoralis major and biceps to help with performing it.

To perform this exercise, grasp the bar with a wide, pronated grip. This exercise begins from a dead-hang (i.e. arms fully extended). When in the bottom position, concentrate on sticking your chest out. Without swinging, pull yourself up until your chin is over the bar. As you pull yourself up, concentrate on pulling your shoulder blades together. This will focus you on training your upper back. Lower yourself until your arms are fully extended and repeat for the desired number of repetitions.

Many will find performing the pull-ups with a close grip and pulling yourself to the front to be the easiest of the three variations. This exercise makes extensive use of the biceps as well as the upper back muscles. Grasp the bar with a close, suppinated grip. Begin this exercise from a dead-hang. Pull yourself up until your chin has cleared the bar.

As with the wide grip to the front variation, stick the chest out in the bottom position and concentrate on bringing the shoulder blades together as you pull yourself up. Avoid swinging.

A spotter may be helpful when performing pull-ups. To spot for this exercise, stand behind the exerciser. To assist, place your hands under his/her shoulder blades and push him/her up. Do not grab the feet or ankles as this will change the mechanics of the exercise and change what muscle groups are being trained.

What if you cannot perform pull-ups? This exercise requires a minimum amount of muscle mass, strength, and technique to perform it. Like with dips (see chapter eleven), the author has not found that people are able to successfully move from an assisted pull-up machine to performing the actual exercise.

A better approach towards building up to being able to perform pull-ups is:

- Increase muscle mass and strength of upper back and biceps muscles. This is best done by performing the exercises described in the rest of this chapter.
- Perform eccentric-only pull-ups. This should be done with the easiest of the three variations (close grip, to the front). When doing these, you should get assistance getting to the top but should fight and take as long as possible to lower yourself down. Focus on correct technique as you lower yourself down.

Lat Pull-Downs

Lat pull-downs are another way to train the muscles of the upper back. They are easier to perform than pull-ups. Pull-downs are easier to add external resistance to. This means they may be able to provide overload more easily than pull-ups. Like pull-ups this exercise will develop the latissimus dorsi, rhomboids, and biceps. There are also several variations possible:

1. wide grip, behind the head;
2. wide grip, to the front; and
3. close grip, to the front, and
4. neutral grip, to the front.

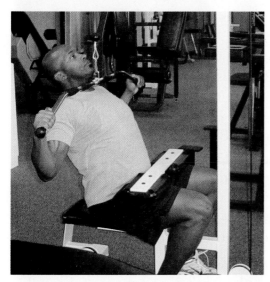

To perform the wide grip, behind the head variation, sit in the bench. You should maintain an upright torso throughout this exercise. Grasp the handles with a wide, pronated grip. Pull the bar behind the body until it touches the base of the neck. Concentrate on squeezing your shoulder blades together while pulling the bar down. Raise the bar under control and repeat.

Do not let the weight lift you out of your seat. You should not lean forward when performing this exercise as this may place your shoulder joint in an unfavorable position. Just like with the pull-up variation of this exercise, individuals with shoulder problems or individuals predisposed to shoulder problems should probably avoid this variation. For the same reasons as the pull ups, this will probably be the most difficult variation of the pull-downs to perform.

To perform the wide grip, pulling the bar to the front variation, sit in the bench. You should maintain an upright torso throughout this exercise. Grasp the handles with a wide, pronated grip. Pull your shoulders back to create a slight arch in your lower back, but do not lean backwards! Pull the bar down in front of your body until it is lower than your chin. Focus on drawing the shoulder blades together as you pull the bar down towards you.

To perform the close grip bringing the bar to the front variation, sit in the bench. Maintain an upright torso throughout this exercise. Grasp the handles with a narrow, suppinated grip. Pull your shoulders back to create a slight arch in your lower back, but do not lean backwards. Pull the bar down in front of your body until the bar is lower than the chin. Again, focus on drawing the shoulder blades together as you pull the bar down.

The final variation involves using a neutral grip, bringing the bar to the front. Grasp the handles and sit in the bench. Pull your shoulders back to create a slight arch in your lower back, but do not lean backwards. Pull the bar down in front of your body until the bar is lower than the chin. Again, focus on drawing the shoulder blades together as you pull the bar down.

When performing pull-downs, make sure that the machine you use holds you securely in place. It is possible to use so much weight on this exercise that the weight can lift you out of your seat!

What's the difference between these variations? Signorile, et al. (2002) did an EMG study looking at these four variations of pull-down. They found the following:

- All variations recruit the latissimus dorsi equally except the pull-downs to the front.

- All variations recruit the pectoralis major and the long head of the triceps to an extent.

- Wide grip pull-downs to the front were the most effective of the four exercises at recruiting the latissimus dorsi, long head of the triceps, and the teres major.

- Wide grip pull-downs to the back are the least effective at recruiting the pectoralis major and the posterior deltoid.

- Close grip pull-downs to the front were the most effective at recruiting the pectoralis major and the long head of the triceps. They were the least effective at recruiting the teres major.

- The neutral grip pull-downs to the front were the least effective at recruiting the long head of the triceps.

Spotting may be useful during pull-downs. Spotting here is used to help you perform extra repetitions. With the first two variations of the pull-down, the spotter should grip the bar inside your hands and help you pull the bar down. With the third variation, the spotter should grip the bar outside your hands and help you pull the bar down. Spotters can also be used to help hold you in the seat if you are handling enough weight to pick you up. This is done by having them grip your traps and push down.

Rows

Rows are to the muscles of the upper back and biceps what the bench press is to the chest and triceps. They are basic, mass- and strength-building exercises for the pulling muscles of the upper body. There are several variations that this chapter will cover:

1. seated rows,
2. bent over rows, and
3. one-arm dumbbell rows.

Seated rows develop the latissimus dorsi, rhomboids, trapezius, posterior deltoids, and biceps. To perform this exercise, take a seated position facing the machine. Place your feet on the machine frame or foot supports. Your knees should be slightly flexed. Grasp the bar handle. The exercise should be started with the torso perpendicular to the floor, chest out, and the arms extended. Without swinging, pull the bar towards the lower chest/upper stomach. Make sure to keep your torso perpendicular to the floor. Keep your elbows next to your ribs while pulling the bar towards your body. As you are pulling the bar towards your body, concentrate on pulling the shoulder blades together.

Seated rows are a great developer of the upper back's musculature. This exercise is not meant to be stressful to the lower back, so it may be a good alternative for people with lower back problems. The most common error seen with this exercise is swinging while performing it. This builds momentum and is a form of cheating. In addition, swinging could injure the lower back. The torso should remain perpendicular to the floor throughout the entire exercise! Just like swinging is bad, so is leaning backward while performing the exercise. This can also place the lower back under strain.

Bent over rows are more difficult than the seated rows and will require more balance, coordination, and flexibility than seated rows. They will also tax the muscles of the lower back. Bent over rows develop the latissimus dorsi, posterior deltoids, rhomboids, trapezius, biceps, and erector spinae.

To perform this exercise, begin with the barbell on the platform. Stand in front of it with your feet approximately hip-width apart. Grasp the bar with a pronated grip that is approximately shoulder width. Stand up with the barbell in your hands. Your knees should be slightly bent. From that position, set your back and then bend forward from your hips. Let the barbell touch your legs at mid-thigh level.

From the starting position pull the barbell up towards your body until it touches your stomach. As you pull the barbell towards you, bring your shoulder blades together and keep your arms against your side. Make sure you do not swing to get the barbell up and concentrate on keeping your back set throughout.

One-arm dumbbell rows are another variation that can be performed which will take stress off the lower back muscles. This variation will develop the latisimus dorsi, rhomboids, posterior deltoids, and biceps.

To perform this exercise, begin with your right knee on a bench. Place your right hand on the bench. Your right arm should be straight. Your trunk should be parallel to the floor. Your left leg should be straight with your left foot on the ground. The dumbbell should be in your left hand and should be in line with your left shoulder. Your left arm should be straight. Concentrate on stretching the latissimus muscle on the left side of your body.

From the start position, moving only your left arm, pull the dumbbell up to the side of your stomach. Concentrate on retracting your shoulder blade and keeping your arm against your body as you pull the dumbbell towards you. When the dumbbell touches your side, lower it back towards the floor and repeat. When the desired number of repetitions have been performed switch sides (i.e. dumbbell in left hand, left foot on floor, right side on bench).

Avoid swinging your body while performing one-arm dumbbell rows. It may allow for more weight to be lifted, but it will defeat the purpose of the exercise. Likewise, concentrate on keeping your trunk parallel to the floor. This will reduce the stress at your lower back.

Shoulder Shrugs

Shoulder shrugs are designed to primarily train the trapezius muscles. To perform this exercise, stand up with the barbell in your hands. The bar should be gripped with a pronated, shoulder-width grip. Your arms should be fully extended. Make sure to set your back before performing the shrug. Raise your shoulders as high as possible. Try to touch your ears with your shoulders. Make sure that you only raise the barbell straight up. Avoid rotating your shoulders.

With shrugs, keep your arms straight throughout the exercise. Force your trapezius to perform the exercise. Make sure to keep your back set throughout, otherwise you can injure your back, you really can work up to a lot of weight on this exercise. Finally, remember to lift the barbell straight up. Rolling your shoulders back to perform the shrug can contribute to shoulder problems over time.

Upright Rows

Upright rows develop the deltoids, trapezius, and elbow flexors. To perform this exercise, stand up and grasp the bar with a pronated grip. Your hands should be shoulder-width apart or a little narrower. Extend your arms fully, so that the bar is touching your thighs. Set your back. From that position, bend your arms and raise the barbell until it is just under your chin. Focus on pulling your elbows straight up.

With upright rows, many lifters will use an extremely narrow grip when performing this exercise. The problem is that when using a narrow grip you do not have much control over the barbell. This exercise should be performed with a shoulder-width grip, or a little narrower. Remember to keep the barbell close to your body while performing this exercise. If you let the bar get away from your body, then the exercise becomes harder to perform. One other common error seen with this exercise includes swinging to get the weight up. This exercise should be performed strictly as swinging may result in a shoulder or lower back injury.

Both shrugs and upright rows can also be performed with dumbbells for variety, the same principles still apply (back set, full range-of-motion, keep the weight close to the body, etc.).

The exercises that have been covered so far are multi-joint exercises that develop the muscles of the upper back and arms. The rest of this chapter will focus on assistance or isolation exercises.

ASSISTANCE EXERCISES

The assistance exercises covered in this chapter are primarily isolation exercises. While important, they should not make up the bulk of a strength and conditioning program. This chapter will cover:

1. biceps curls, and
2. wrist curls.

Biceps Curls

Biceps curls are meant to develop those muscles which flex the elbow; the biceps, brachioradialis, brachialis, and even the forearm (wrist flexor/extensor, pronators/suppinators) muscles. There are many possible variations of curls that may be performed, this chapter will cover two: barbell curls and dumbbell curls.

Barbell curls develop the biceps, brachioradialis, and forearm muscles. To perform this exercise, stand up with the barbell in your hands. Grip the bar with a suppinated grip, your hands should be approximately shoulder-width apart. Your arms should begin the exercise fully extended and should be at your sides. From the starting position, flex your elbows and curl the weight up towards your shoulders. Lower the weight back to the starting position in a slow, controlled manner.

When performing this exercise, your elbows should remain against your sides throughout. Moving your elbows forward or backward will involve your shoulder muscles and take some of the emphasis off your biceps. Avoid swinging or leaning backward while curling as this could hurt your lower back. Some people will experience wrist pain while performing this exercise. This could be due to flexing the wrist while curling.

Performing curls with dumbbells allows you to turn your wrist while performing the exercise, which will bring more muscles into play. Curls with dumbbells will develop the biceps, brachioradialis, brachialis, and forearms.

To perform this exercise, grasp a dumbbell in each hand. This exercise can be performed while standing or while sitting. This exercise uses a neutral grip, i.e. your palms should face your body. Begin this exercise with both your arms fully extended. Using one arm at a time (or both arms at the same time) curl the dumbbell towards your shoulder. As you curl the weight, you should turn your hand so that it becomes supinated (i.e. by the time the dumbbell reaches your shoulder you hand should be supinated). Just like with barbell curls, swinging or leaning should be avoided during this exercise.

Wrist Curls

Wrist curls focus on those muscles that flex or extend the wrist joint. There are many possible variations of wrist curls, this chapter will focus on barbell wrist curls and barbell reverse wrist curls.

Barbell wrist curls develop the wrist flexors. To perform barbell wrist curls, sit on a bench and hold a barbell with a close, supinated grip. Both forearms should rest on the bench with the wrist, hand, and barbell unsupported by the bench. Relax the wrists until they are fully extended. From that position, keeping your forearms on the bench, flex your wrists and curl the barbell towards you.

Barbell reverse wrist curls develop the wrist extensors and are a more difficult exercise than wrist curls. To perform this exercise, sit in front of a bench and rest your forearms on it. You should be gripping a barbell with a pronated grip. Relax your wrists until they are fully flexed. From that position, keeping your forearms on the bench, extend your wrists and curl the barbell towards you.

CORE EXERCISES

The "core" refers to the abdominal muscles and the lower back muscles. These muscles are extremely important for a number of reasons. First, they act to stabilize the pelvis and spine. This serves to prevent injuries. Second, strong core muscles allow one to maintain good posture. This is important because in athletics, force is transferred most effectively from the lower body to the upper body through a straight line. Finally, as was hinted at in the last item, strong core muscles allow one to transfer force from the lower body to the upper body.

This chapter will be divided into four parts: abdominal exercises, lower back exercises, stability ball exercises, and stabilization exercises.

ABDOMINAL EXERCISES

Many people feel that just by performing abdominal work they can reduce the fat in their stomach. This idea is called *spot reduction.* According to McArdle, Katch, and Katch (1996), there is no evidence that spot reduction takes place (i.e. sit-ups will not make your stomach smaller). With regards to spot reduction and core training, it is important to realize two things. First, weight training (and abdominal exercise) does not use fat for fuel. Second, when fat is lost through a combination of diet and exercise, it is done across the entire body, and usually from the areas of greatest fat concentration.

Abdominal exercises are important to perform because abdominal fitness may contribute to preventing or rehabilitating lower back injury.

This chapter is organized a little bit differently from the other exercise chapters. This chapter is organized around the idea of progression. That is, for many of the exercises a number of variations are presented. These are presented from the "easiest" version and gradually increase in difficulty. This is being done because some of these exercises can be potentially harmful to the lower back if they are done before an adequate level of muscular fitness exists. Those individuals who do not have a high level of fitness, or who have a lower back injury, should probably start with the exercises having the least amount of difficulty and progress slowly.

In general, the following progressions will be used on the abdominal exercises:

1. partial movements to full movements,
2. body-weight exercises to exercises with added weight, and
3. slow speed exercises to explosive exercises.

This part of the chapter will be grouped into four sections; crunches, sit-ups, exercises for the obliques, and leg raises. With any of the exercises in this chapter, keep in mind that these exercises are not supposed to hurt your lower back. If you are experiencing low back pain from these exercises, then you should stop performing them and see your doctor!

The Abdominal Crunch

The abdominal crunch is one of the most effective exercises for working the upper abdominal muscles. In fact, it is as effective or more effective than much of the equipment you can buy from sporting goods stores and infomercials. It is also one of the least stressful exercises to the lower back.

This exercise will be divided into several progressions. These progressions, organized from least difficult to most difficult are:

1. crunch with arms at the side,
2. abdominal crunch,
3. abdominal crunch with weight on the chest, and
4. abdominal crunch with weight overhead.

To perform the crunch with your arms at your side, lie down on your back. Your knees should be bent to allow your feet to be in contact with the ground. Your arms should be extended next to your body. From this position, lift your hips up slightly to flatten out your lower back.

From the starting position, tense up your abdominal muscles and lift your shoulder blades off the ground. As this happens your hands should move forward towards your feet. Hold this position for approximately three seconds and return to the starting position with your shoulders touching the ground.

To perform the abdominal crunch, assume the same starting position as the crunch with arms at the side. Cross your arms over your chest. Your right hand should grasp your left shoulder and your left hand should grasp your right shoulder. From this position, lift your hips up slightly to flatten your lower back. From the starting position, tense up your abdominal muscles and lift your shoulder blades off the ground. Hold this position for approximately three seconds then return to the starting position with your shoulders touching the ground.

The crunch with weight on your chest begins with the same starting position as the abdominal crunch. Place a dumbbell across your chest so that it touches either shoulder. Cross your arms over the dumbbell. Your right hand should grasp the left end of the dumbbell and your left hand should grasp the right end of the dumbbell. Tense up your abdominal muscles and lift your shoulder blades off the ground. You should lift yourself up until your shoulders are no longer in contact with the ground. Hold this position then return to the starting position.

The abdominal crunch with weight overhead is the most difficult of the crunch variations and perhaps the most stressful to the lower back. Extend your arms over your head and hold a weight in your hands. Keep your arms straight. From this position, lift your hips up slightly to flatten out your lower back. Tense up your abdominal muscles and lift your shoulder blades off the ground. Maintain the weight overhead on straight arms. Hold this position and then return to the starting position.

A few words of caution about abdominal crunches and their variations; first, some people will complain of neck pain while performing these exercises. If this is the case, focus on trying to touch the chin to the chest to relax the neck muscles while performing the crunch. Second, the technical pointer about lifting the hips up slightly is very important particularly for individuals with lower back problems. By lifting the hips up, the lower back will flatten which will reduce some of the stress experienced by the lower back.

The Sit-Up

The sit-up has fallen out of favor in recent years because it does not isolate the abdominal muscles as well as the crunch does. Some of this has to do with mechanics. During abdominal exercises, the first and last 30-45 degrees of the movement is the responsibility of the abdominal muscles, with the middle parts of the movement being the responsibility of the hip flexors. The reason crunches are better at "isolating" the abdominal muscles is because a crunch only works the first and last 30-45 degrees of the movement. Sit-ups, on the other hand, work the entire range of motion. So not only are the abdominal muscles involved but so are the hip flexors.

The drawback to sit-ups is that they generate high compressive forces at the lumbar spine. In individuals with a good degree of fitness this is not a problem, but in individuals without that fitness this could lead to back problems. It is recommended that if you are not already active, if you do not already have a good degree of abdominal fitness, or if you have a lower back injury then you should begin with the crunch exercise and save sit-ups until you have a higher degree of fitness.

This exercise will be divided into several progressions. These progressions, organized from least difficult to most difficult are:

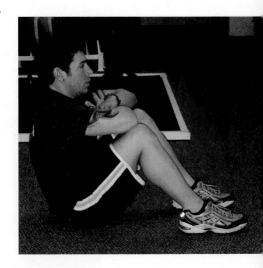

1. sit-ups,
2. sit-ups with weight,
3. sit-ups with weight overhead, and
4. sit-ups with a medicine ball toss.

To perform the sit-up, lie down on your back. Your knees should be bent to allow your feet to be in contact with the ground. You may need someone or something to secure your feet. Your arms should be crossed over your chest. Sit up until your elbows touch your knees. Return to the starting position with your shoulders touching the ground and repeat.

To perform the sit-up with weight, assume the starting position for the sit-up described above. Hold the weight on your chest. Once again, your arms should be crossed across your chest. Sit up until your elbows touch your knees. Lower yourself back to the starting position and repeat.

To perform the sit-up with weight overhead, assume the starting position for the sit-up. Hold the weight over your head on straight arms (just like in the crunch exercise). Keeping the weight overhead on straight arms, sit up. Return to the starting position with your shoulders touching the ground and repeat. This variation is designed to prepare you to perform the exercise with a medicine ball toss.

The sit-up with a medicine ball toss makes the sit-up explosive. This is best performed in a bench that will secure your feet. Lie on the bench and bend your knees. Secure your feet under the restraints. Tighten your stomach muscles and raise your arms straight over your head. Begin this exercise in the up position. You will need to have a partner standing in front of the bench holding a medicine ball (see photo 13-9). Your partner should throw the medicine ball to your hands. Immediately upon catching the ball, perform a fast, explosive sit-up. As you complete the sit-up, throw the ball back to your partner.

A few words of caution about these exercises, first, keep your abdominal muscles tight throughout. This will help reduce some of the strain to your lower back. Second, do not bounce off the bench or the ground in the low position. This will also defeat the purpose of the exercise.

To make sit-ups more difficult, perform them on an incline bench. The greater the incline, the greater the degree of difficulty. They may also be performed on an unstable surface (e.g. a stability ball) to increase their difficulty, this will be discussed in more detail later in this chapter.

Exercises for the Obliques

The above exercises are all well and good, but what works the obliques? Believe it or not, the oblique muscles actually appear to be involved in the crunch, sit up, and leg raise (especially the hanging straight leg raises). However, this section will also present some other exercises to target the obliques.

These exercises, organized from least difficult to most difficult are:

1. cross-knee crunch,

2. twisting sit-up,

3. twisting sit-up with medicine ball, and

4   twisting sit-up with medicine ball toss.

To perform the cross knee crunch, lie down on your back. Your knees should be bent to allow your feet to be in contact with the ground. Your left

leg should be crossed over your right. Your right hand should be behind your head. From the starting position, tense your abdominal muscles and lift your shoulder blades off the ground. As your shoulder blades lift off the ground, twist gently so that your right elbow moves towards your left thigh. Hold this position for approximately three seconds. Return to the starting position and repeat this movement for the other side.

To perform twisting sit-ups, lie down on your back and assume the starting position for the sit-up described above. Sit up, raising your shoulders and lower back off the ground. As you raise yourself off the ground, twist gently so that your left elbow moves towards your right knee. Then twist so that your right elbow moves towards your left knee. Return to the starting position and repeat this movement for the other side.

The twisting sit-up with a medicine ball is best performed on a bench that will allow you to secure your feet while performing the exercise. Sit down on the bench and secure your feet under the restraints. Begin this exercise in the up position. Hold a medicine ball straight out in front of you, level with your chest. From this position, twist to your right side as you lie down towards the bench. The medicine ball should move to your right side as you twist your body. Lie down until your right shoulder touches the bench. From this position reverse directions until you are sitting straight up again with the ball held out in front of you. Repeat this motion but on the left side. This exercise is designed to prepare you for the explosive version (e.g. with medicine ball toss).

The twisting sit-up with a medicine ball toss makes the twisting sit-up explosive. This is best performed in a bench that will secure your feet. Lie on the bench and bend your knees. Secure your feet under the restraints. Tighten your stomach muscles and hold your arms straight in front of you at chest level. Begin this exercise in the up position. You will need to have a partner standing in front of the bench holding a medicine ball. Your partner should throw the medicine ball to your side. Immediately twist to the side and catch the ball, following it through until your shoulder touches the bench. Perform an explosive sit-up and throw the ball back to your partner as you sit up and straighten out.

With the oblique exercises it is important to concentrate on several things. First, keep your abdominal muscles tight. This will help reduce some of the strain to your lower back. Second, refrain from bouncing or using momentum to perform the exercises. Not only will this defeat the purpose of the exercise but it will also increase the stress and strain experienced by the lower back.

The Leg Raise

Leg raises can be among the most effective abdominal exercises - for upper, lower, and even oblique abdominal muscles. However, these exercises (when done lying down) can also produce some of the greatest compression at the lower back.

Beginners should start with the abdominal crunch exercises, then progress to sit-ups, and finally after they have developed a foundation of fitness begin performing leg raises.

This exercise will be divided into several progressions. These progressions, organized from least difficult to most difficult are:

1. lying, bent leg raise;
2. lying, straight leg raise;
3. hanging, bent leg raise; and
4. hanging, straight leg raise.

To perform lying bent leg raises, lie flat on your back. Your legs should be bent at the knees and your feet should be flat on the floor. Place your hands under your buttocks for support. From the starting position, raise your knees until you have a 90 degree angle at the hips. All of the movement should come from your hips during this exercise.

Lying straight leg raises begin with you lying flat on your back. Your legs should be completely extended. Place your hands under your buttocks for support. Moving from your hips, raise your legs off the ground several inches. Focus on keeping your abdominal muscles tight throughout the performance of this exercise. Some trainees will swing when performing this exercise, this is usually due to a combination of weak abdominals and lifting the legs too high during the leg raises.

To perform hanging bent leg raises, grip a pull up bar with a pronated grip. Hang from the bar so that your feet are not in contact with the ground. Your arms and legs should be completely extended. Moving from your hips, bring your legs straight up in front of you. As you reach the top position of this exercise, concentrate on flexing your trunk to aid you with brining your abdominal muscles into this exercise. Avoid swinging during this exercise. Wrist straps will aid greatly with your grip during this exercise.

Hanging straight leg raises begin in the same manner as the hanging bent leg raise. Grip a pull up bar with a pronated grip. Hang from the bar so that your feet are not in contact with the ground. Your arms and legs should be completely extended. Moving from your hips, bring your legs straight up in front of you. Bring your legs up until they are parallel to the ground. As you raise your legs, concentrate on flexing your trunk so that you may bring your abdominal muscles into the exercise. Do not swing during this exercise.

LOWER BACK EXERCISES

The exercises in this section are designed to train the muscles of the lower back. Each of them will also train the hamstring muscles. Due to how each exercise is performed, it is important that you observe proper back management when performing these exercises. This is more important than the amount of weight you can lift. Failure to observe proper lifting mechanics can result in a major injury from these exercises.

This chapter will discuss the following lower back exercises:

- good mornings,
- stiff legged deadlifts,

- back extensions, and
- reverse hyperextensions.

Good Mornings

Good mornings develop the erector spinae, hamstrings, and gluteal muscles. They are performed standing up. To perform good mornings, stand with the barbell behind your neck, resting on your shoulders. Grip the bar with a pronated grip. Position your feet between hip- and shoulder-width apart. Unlock your knees (i.e. there should be a slight bend in your knees throughout the exercise). From this position, set your back. Perform this exercise by pushing your hips back. This will cause your torso to incline forward. Bend forward from your hips until your torso is parallel to the floor. Once in the bottom position, extend your hips until you are standing straight up again.

Remember that all of the movement in this exercise should come from your hips! It is absolutely critical that you keep your back set throughout this exercise. This exercise is great for strengthening the lower back and hamstrings. However, you should be cautious on this exercise and use light weights when performing it for the first time. Advance slowly and cautiously on this exercise. Too much weight, too soon, and you could end up hurt.

Stiff-Legged Deadlifts

Stiff-legged deadlifts are a popular hamstring and lower back exercise. However, they also develop the gluteal muscles. To perform them, start out with the barbell on the floor. Grasp the barbell with a pronated grip. You should grip the bar with a slightly wider than shoulder-width grip. Your arms should be straight during this exercise. Stand up with the barbell in your hands. You should have a slight bend in your knees. Set you back. Keeping your back set, bend forward by pushing your hips back. As your hips are pushed back, your torso should incline forward. Moving from your hips, bend forward as far as you comfortably can. Once you've gone as far as you can, reverse direction until you are standing upright again. Keep the bar close to your body throughout.

It is important that all the movement in this exercise come from your hips. This is to insure that this exercise works what it is supposed to. Performing this exercise with a set back means that you may not be able to bend forward very far - that's okay. Your flexibility will increase from this exercise. Remember to keep a slight bend in the knees. You do not want to lock out your knees on this exercise.

Back Extensions

This exercise is performed in a "hyperextension bench." It is also known as a hyperextension or as a back raise. It is designed to train the muscles of your lower back and hamstrings. To perform this exercise, lie face down in the bench. The back of your ankles should be restrained under the pads of the bench. The front of your thighs should also be on the bench. From this position, bending at your hips, lower yourself as far as is comfortable. Keep your back set (i.e. their should be a straight line running from your shoulders to your hips) and use your hips as a pivot point for the movement. From the starting position, using your lower back and hamstrings, raise your upper body until it is extended. Repeat.

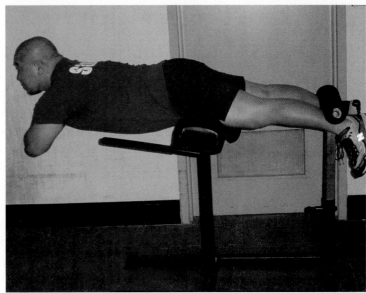

Reverse Hyperextensions

Reverse hyperextensions are another exercise to target the hamstring, glutes, and lower back muscles. They can be performed on a bench press or other flat bench. To perform this exercise, lie face down on the bench. Your hips and legs should be off the bench and your legs should be straight. Keeping your upper body on the bench and your legs straight, raise them behind you until they are parallel to the floor. Lower and repeat. With this exercise, a few things should be kept in mind. First, keep the upper body on the bench. Beginners have a tendency to try to use the upper body to cheat, this usually looks like they are flopping around on the bench! Second, it is helpful to keep the legs together while raising and lowering them.

STABILITY BALL EXERCISES

Stability ball exercises involve performing exercises on a large, inflated ball. These exercises have traditionally been used in rehab and have lately crossed over into mainstream fitness. In theory, performing exercises on a large inflated ball poses a number of challenges. First, you must perform the exercise, which will allow you to train specific muscles. Second, you must remain on the ball. This can be difficult while trying to perform exercises. Third, you must keep the ball in place; this is necessary because large round balls have a tendency to roll away! The combination of these things are believed to recruit more muscles (especially in the body's core) than performing the exercises on the flat, stable ground. There is some research to support this, although this is an area that needs more.

Due to the inherent challenges with performing exercises on a large, inflated ball, there are a series of progressions that can be used to help teach the skill that is necessary to safely and effectively perform stability ball exercises. This section will cover progressions for the following classes of stability ball exercises:

- seated,
- supine, and
- prone.

Seated Stability Ball Exercises

Exercises performed while sitting on the stability ball will be the easiest for many people to perform. The goal behind these exercises is to get you comfortable with balancing on the ball. The following seated exercises, each are progressively more difficult then the one preceding it, will be covered in this section:

1. Bounce
2. Shift your weight
3. Sit-ups
4. Seated twists
5. Twisting sit-ups
6. Leg extensions
7. Leg curls
8. Leg raises

The bounce exercise is meant to get you comfortable with sitting on the ball. Sit on the ball. Ideally the ball size should be selected so that your thighs are close to parallel to the floor. Tense the abdominal muscles and sit tall (chest out, shoulders back) on the ball. Place your hands on your hips. From this position, simply bounce up and down in a controlled manner.

Shifting your weight teaches you to balance on the ball while moving. Assume the same starting position as in the bounce exercise. Once you are

sitting tall and keeping your feet in place shift your hips to the right. Now shift them to the left. Keeping your feet in place shift your hips forwards, then backwards. Make a circle with the stability ball by moving your hips (keep your feet in place).

Sit-ups reinforce comfort and balance while developing the core muscles. Sit tall on the ball, walk forward a few steps so that you are reclining on the ball slightly. Cross your hands over your chest and perform sit-ups. Try to avoid performing this exercise by thrusting the hips.

Seated twists continue reinforcing comfort and balance on the ball while further developing the core muscles. Sit tall on the ball and extend your arms straight out in front of you. Keeping the ball stationary, turn your shoulders to your left. Turn your shoulders to the right. Make these movements slow and controlled, do not allow momentum to help.

Twisting sit-ups are a more advanced exercise and combine sit-ups and seated twists. Begin the exercise in the same position as the sit-up. Perform a sit-up. As you are sitting up, twist to the left side and then to the right. Keep the ball in place and move in a controlled manner.

The leg extension exercise requires you to balance on one leg at a time while keeping control of the ball. Sit tall on the ball. From this position, keeping the ball stationary, extend your right knee until your leg is parallel to the ground. Repeat with the other leg. Once you are comfortable with this movement, it can be performed with leg weights or against tubing or bands.

The leg curl exercise requires resistance. Sit tall on the ball and extend the right knee so that the right leg is parallel to the ground. Apply resistance behind the right heel. Keeping the ball stationary, try to flex the right leg against the resistance. Repeat with the other side.

The leg raise exercise is the most difficult of these exercise progressions. Sit tall on the ball and extend the right knee. Keeping the ball in place, raise the entire leg up and down moving from your hip. Switch sides.

Supine Stability Ball Exercises

Once you are comfortable with sitting on the ball, it is time to go somewhere with the ball to perform the next exercises. Supine stability ball exercises all begin from a seated position and progress to the supine position. The following exercises will be covered (they are listed in the order that they should be mastered):

1. Walk-outs
2. Crunches
3. Cross-knee crunches
4. Leg extensions
5. Leg curls
6. Leg raises

Walk-outs teach how to move into the supine position. Begin sitting tall on the ball. From that position, walk the feet forward allowing your body to slide along the ball. Walk forward until the ball is under the shoulder blades. From that position walk back until you are sitting tall on the ball again.

For crunches, walk out until the ball is either in the small of the back or under the shoulder blades. Cross the arms across the chest, tense the abdominal muscles, and perform crunches by lifting the shoulder blades off the ball. Lock the hips into place so that the exercise is not being performed by hip thrusts.

For cross-knee crunches, walk out into the same starting position as the crunch. Place the hands behind the head. Perform a crunch, as you are lifting your shoulder blades off the ball twist so that the right elbow moves towards the left side. Repeat with the other side. Make sure to keep the ball in place throughout this exercise.

Leg extensions reduce stability by forcing you to balance on one leg. Walk out until the ball is under your shoulder blades. From that position, extend the right knee until the lower leg is parallel to the floor. Repeat and then switch sides.

Like with the seated variation, leg curls require that you extend your knee and then attempt to flex it against resistance.

Leg raises are performed exactly as they are in the seated variation, except they are done after walking out until the ball is under the shoulder blades.

Prone Stability Ball Exercises

Prone stability ball exercises are a little different because they are performed face down and ultimately with the feet on the ball. The following progressions will be covered in this chapter:

1. Walk-outs
2. Leg raises
3. Push-ups
4. Lift arm

Walk-outs are designed to get your comfortable with the prone position. Begin on all fours with the ball under your stomach. From this position, walk forward with the hands. As you walk forward, allow your body to slide over the ball until the ball is located under your feet. From that position walk backwards and repeat.

Leg raises require you to learn how to stabilize your body while your feet are on the ball. Walk out until the ball is under your feet. From that position, keeping your leg straight, perform leg raises by lifting your right leg off the ball. Switch sides.

For push-ups, walk out until the ball is under your feet. From that position perform push-ups, making sure to balance on the ball. For added difficulty, lift one leg off the ball while performing the push-ups.

Lifting the arm will be the most challenging variation for most people. Walk out until the ball is under your feet. After stabilizing yourself, raise your right arm straight out in front of you. Repeat and then switch sides. For added difficulty, when lifting the right arm try to lift the left leg of the ball and vice versa.

STABILIZATION EXERCISES

Stabilization exercises have become popular in recent years. These exercises do not require as much skill, strength, or muscular fitness as many of the exercises described previously in this chapter. It is easy to have large groups perform them (such as a football team, physical education class, etc.). They do not require much time and they work most of the muscles of the core. This section will cover three variations:

- prone holds,
- side holds, and
- supine holds.

Prone Holds

To perform the prone hold lie face down on the ground. You should support yourself on your toes and your forearms. If this is done correctly, there should be a straight line between your ankles and your shoulders (i.e. your hips should not sag or be pushed up into the air). Hold this position for the desired amount of time.

To make this exercise more difficult, assume the prone hold position. From here perform straight leg raises with your right leg, then your left. To add still more difficulty, perform the exercise with your forearms on an unstable surface such as a stability ball or a balance disc.

Side Hold

To perform the side hold, lie on your right side. Raise yourself up so that your weight is supported only by your right forearm and the outside of your right foot. If this is done correctly then your body should be straight between your feet and your shoulders. Hold this position for the desired amount of time and then switch sides.

To make this exercise more difficult, assume the side hold position on your right side. From here perform a straight leg raise with your left leg. Switch sides. Again, this exercise can also be performed on an unstable surface.

Supine Hold

For the supine hold, sit on the ground and place your hands flat on the ground behind your hips. Extend your arms so that they are straight. As you do this, extend your legs until just your heels and your hands are in contact with the ground. Done correctly there should be a straight line between your ankles and your shoulders.

For added difficulty leg raises may be performed, or the hands (or heels) may be placed on an unstable surface.

14 TOTAL BODY EXERCISE

The exercises covered in this chapter are difficult to classify in terms of what muscles they emphasize. This is because these exercises work just about every muscle in the body during some phase of the lift. The exercises in this chapter, along with the multi-joint exercises described over the previous several chapters, should form the backbone of a strength and conditioning program. These exercises develop total body strength, mobility, balance, and power.

This chapter will cover the following exercises:

■ the deadlift,
■ the power clean,
■ the power jerk, and
■ the power snatch.

THE DEADLIFT

The deadlift is an exercise that involves picking a weight up off the floor and standing up with it. As a result, it is an excellent conditioning exercise for the lower extremities and core muscles.

There are two primary types of deadlift: using a wider grip and a narrow foot stance, called a conventional deadlift, and using a narrower grip and a wider foot stance, called a sumo deadlift. This chapter will discuss both types of deadlifts as well as other variations that may be performed.

Conventional Deadlifts

With conventional deadlifts, the exercise begins with the barbell on the platform. Stand in front of the bar with your feet approximately hip-width apart. Squat down so that you attempt to put your stomach between your legs and grip the bar with a mixed grip. Your hands should be approximately shoulder-width apart. As you squat down, set your back and look straight ahead. If this is done properly, your hips should be higher than your knees, the bar should be pulled against your shins, your shoulders should be in front of the bar, and your arms should be straight.

Lift the barbell off the platform by extending your hips and knees. As you do this focus on several things. First, keep your arms straight. Failure to do this could lead to a biceps injury, as the biceps is not meant to lift as much weight as you can deadlift. Second, keep the bar close to your body. Not only does this protect your lower back but it makes the bar easier to lift. Third, make sure your hips and shoulders travel up at the same speed. Failing to do this can place too much stress on the lower back. Fourth, keep your back set. Finally, keep your shoulders in front of the barbell.

When the bar has reached mid-thigh level, extend your hips and straighten out with the bar in your hands. During this portion of the lift, your shoulders will move from being in front of the bar to being behind it. At the completion of this part of the deadlift, you should be standing up straight, chest high, shoulders back, and arms straight.

The conventional deadlift is ideal for people with longer arms. The sumo deadlift, on the other hands, is ideal for people with shorter arms and tends to emphasize the quadriceps more and the lower back less.

Sumo Deadlifts

This exercise also begins with the barbell on the platform. With this variation, approach the bar and stand so that your feet are shoulder-width apart or a little wider. You should take a mixed grip on the bar, with your hands closer together than hip-width apart. Squat down and grip the bar. Focus on keeping your back set during this exercise. You will be more upright at the start than in the conventional deadlift (i.e. your hips may be lower than in the conventional deadlift).

From the start, extend your legs and hips until you are standing up with the bar in your hands. At the top, you should be standing up straight, with your chest elevated and your shoulders back. Remember to keep your arms straight.

In addition to the conventional and sumo deadlifts, there are a few other variations that may be performed. These may be used for variety or to train parts of the lifts.

Deadlift Variations

This chapter will describe two variations of the deadlift, each of which can be performed either sumo or conventionally:

- deadlift to the knees, and
- deadlift lockouts.

The deadlift to the knees is meant to strengthen the part of the lift that involves picking the bar up off the platform. This will be particularly helpful to conventional deadlifters who are frequently weaker during this phase. To perform this variation, lift the bar until it reaches knee height. At this point set the barbell back down and repeat. Focus on perfect technique with every repetition.

Deadlift lockouts are meant to strengthen the last part of the lift, generally from mid-thigh to standing up. This is usually performed in a squat rack. Adjust the rack so that the bar is at mid-thigh level. Set yourself up as if you had lifted the bar to mid-thigh level. From that position complete the pull. Focus on perfect technique and do not allow yourself to bounce the bar in the squat rack.

THE POWER CLEAN

The power clean is a total body exercise that develops explosiveness. It is used extensively in the training of weightlifters and athletes. This exercise involves exerting force against the ground, using the entire body to accomplish it and performing the exercise quickly. It is also performed standing up. For these reasons, it is felt to have a great deal of transfer to the playing field. This chapter will discuss how to perform the power clean, what common errors to avoid, and how to perform variations of this exercise.

The power clean is divided into several phases:

1. the start, where you interact with the barbell while it is on the platform;
2. the first pull, where the barbell is lifted to knee height;
3. the second pull, where the barbell achieves its maximum velocity;
4. the nonsupport phase, where you are not in contact with the ground as you lift the barbell to its maximum height;
5. the amortization phase, where you drop under the barbell and "catch" it on the front of your shoulders; and
6. the finish, where you stand up with the barbell on the front of your shoulders.

Power Clean Technique

Begin the power clean with the barbell on the platform. Approach the bar and stand in front of it so that your feet are approximately hip-width apart. Squat down and grip the bar with a pronated grip. Your grip width should be approximately shoulder-width apart (you should use the same grip width that you use on the front squat).

Once you have gripped the bar, squat down and attempt to put your stomach between your legs. As you do this take a deep breath, hold it, and set your back. Your shoulders should be just in front of the barbell, with your arms straight and your elbows rotated out. Rotating your elbows out will help you to

keep your arms straight during the performance of the power clean. If all this is done correctly then your hips will be higher than your knees in the starting position.

Lifting the barbell to knee height (i.e. the first pull) should be done in a slow, controlled manner. This is because ripping the barbell off the platform may result in the making of "small" technique errors that may have major consequences later on in the lift. To perform the first pull, extend your knees and hips to lift the barbell. Your hips and shoulders should travel up at the same speed. During the first pull, as your knees extend, the barbell should move back towards your body a few centimeters. If the first pull is done properly, then your shoulders will remain in front of the bar. Your arms should remain straight and your back should remain set.

The next part of the lift is the second pull. The second pull is the phase of the exercise where the barbell reaches its maximum velocity and is the explosive part of the lift. When the bar reaches the height of the knees, continue extending your knees until the barbell scrapes your thighs. Once the bar has scraped your thighs, extend your hips violently and rise up on your toes while shrugging your shoulders up. During the second pull, your shoulders will move from being in front of the barbell to being behind it. If the second pull is done properly, then the force imparted to the bar will force it to move up the body.

The second pull will force the bar to reach its maximum height (which should be around chest level). Once the bar has reached chest level, begin bending your arms to prepare you to drop under the bar. As this happens move your feet to the sides slightly. You should be preparing to move your feet from hip-width to shoulder-width apart to allow you a more stable base with which to the catch the bar.

As you move your feet to the sides in the nonsupport phase, pull yourself under the bar. This will require you to rotate your elbows around the bar so that you may catch it on the front of your shoulders. You should receive the bar on the front of your shoulders at the same time you "land" in a $1/4$ squat. This position should be similar to a front squat, i.e. back set, chest out, elbows high, hips pushed back, knees bent.

Once the bar has been received on the front of the shoulders, extend your knees and hips until you are standing straight up. Make sure to keep your chest out, shoulders back, and your elbows high.

There are a number of common errors to avoid with the power clean. These are going to be discussed by the phase of the lift that they occur in.

- *The start:* The most common error associated with the start is not having your back set. This can result in a dangerous pulling position for your lower back.
- *The first pull:* As with the start, one of the common errors is to pull with a rounded back. Another error is to have the hips travel up faster than the shoulders. This tends to cause an "action-reaction" to occur with the bar. Lifting the hips up too quickly results in the bar being thrown away from the body during the second pull which makes it very difficult to control.
- *The second pull:* One common error seen during the second pull is to perform it in parts. This results in less power being generated so that barbell does not achieve as much height or velocity. Another error is to use the arms too soon to try to pull the barbell. This will slow down the lift and make it more difficult. A final error is to thrust the hips forward, instead of simply extending them. Thrusting the hips forward forces the barbell away from the body, making it more difficult to control.
- *The nonsupport/amortization phase:* One of the biggest errors here is to split the feet too far to the sides during this phase. They should not be moved further than shoulder-width apart. Moving the feet too wide can make balance difficult.

The power clean has many variations that may be performed. These may be done for variety, they may be done to work on certain phases of the lift, or they may be done to develop certain qualities or muscle groups.

Power Clean Variations

This chapter will cover a number of variations that are possible with the power clean. These variations include:

- power cleans from the hang,
- power cleans from blocks, and
- clean pulls.

The power clean from the hang is designed to do a number of things. First, it develops technique by emphasizing portions of the lift. Second, it develops back strength due to the fact that you must hold the bar in the starting positions. Third, each clean from the hang has a second pull, so it will enhance explosiveness.

There are three primary variations possible with the power clean from the hang. It may be performed with the barbell starting out above the knees. It may be performed with the barbell starting out at knee height. It may also be performed with the barbell starting out at below the knee height.

To perform the power clean from the hang, with the barbell above the knees, begin by taking a clean-width grip on the barbell and standing up with it in your hands. Your feet should be hip-width apart. Set your back. From this position, push your hips back and unlock your knees. Do this until the bar reaches the middle of your thighs. From that position, keeping your arms straight, perform a slight dip with your knees and then execute the power clean. This variation is slightly more difficult than the power clean from the floor because there is not time to generate as much force as when you are lifting it from the floor.

To perform the power clean from the hang, with the barbell at knee height, begin by standing up with the barbell in your hands. Unlock your knees and push your hips back until the bar reaches mid-thigh. At this point, continue pushing your hips back and bend your knees until you lower the bar to knee height. From this point perform the power clean. Focus on pulling the bar close to your body as it passes knee height.

To perform the power clean from the hang, with the barbell at below the knee height, begin by standing up with the barbell in your hands. As previously described, lower the bar until it reaches knee height. Continue lowering the bar until it is below your knees. From this point perform the power clean. This is often the most difficult variation to learn as many people have trouble moving the barbell past the knees.

Like the power cleans from the hang, power cleans from blocks may also be performed from above the knee height, from knee height, and from below knee height. With this variation, the bar begins on a raised stands. This means that one does not need to posses the same amount of back strength to perform this variation. With the exception of the barbell beginning on a raised stand, the exercise is performed just like it is from the hang.

Clean pulls may be performed from the hang or from blocks. They may be performed from the floor, from above the knees, from the knees, and from below the knees. Clean pulls are an exercise designed to train the first and second pulls (depending upon which variation is performed).

To perform a clean pull from the floor, set up just like you were going to perform the power clean. Perform the first and second pulls just like you were going to perform a power clean. However, stop the exercise after the second pull. In other words, shrug your shoulder up violently as you extend your hips and rise up on your toes. From this position lower the barbell back to the floor and repeat the exercise. Do not hold the top position. This exercise is meant to develop strength and explosiveness. It is also extremely useful to athletes because it does not require as much technique as the power clean.

To perform the variations from the hang or from blocks, perform them just like the power clean only stop after the second pull.

THE POWER JERK

The power jerk is an explosive, total-body exercise that heavily involves the muscles of the upper body. This is a great exercise for throwers, football players, and baseball players who must be able to use the muscles of their upper body explosively. This section will discuss how to perform the power jerk, what common errors to avoid, and how to perform variations of this exercise.

The power jerk is divided into several phases:

1. the start, where the barbell is resting on the front of your shoulders;
2. the dip, where you squat down with the bar on the front of your shoulders;
3. the drive, where you extend your hips and knees and push the bar off your shoulders;
4. the squat under, where you drop under the bar and "catch" it at arm's length; and
5. the finish, where you stand up with the bar overhead.

Power Jerk Technique

Begin this exercise with the bar on the front of your shoulders. This may be accomplished by taking it from a squat rack or by cleaning it to your shoulders. Take a pronated grip on the bar, with a clean-width grip. From this position stand up straight, take a deep breath, and hold it. Set your back. Your feet should be hip-width apart.

From the starting position, quickly squat down into a ¼ squat. As you do this make sure to hold the bar on your shoulders. Keep your weight on your heels and remember to squat by pushing your hips back and then bending your knees.

Without pausing at the bottom of the dip, reverse direction and drive up powerfully with your legs. The faster you can switch from the dip to the drive the more elastic potential will be created in your lower body and the more force you can impart to the bar. Drive up onto your toes. This should force the bar off your shoulders.

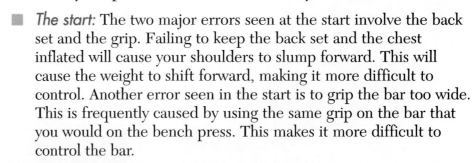

When the bar has reached its maximum height (usually eye level) move your feet to the sides so that they end up shoulder-width apart. When your feet land on the ground you should bend your knees and catch the bar in a ¼ squat. The combination of moving your feet and squatting will move you underneath the bar enabling you to catch it at arms' length. When you catch the bar your arms must be locked out. The bar does not travel straight up. It should travel up and slightly behind the head. To make the bar easier to control, it should be in line with your hips when catching it overhead. Placing it too far forward or too far back will result in difficulty controlling the bar.

From the ¼ squat, stand up with the weight overhead. Keep your arms locked out throughout and keep the bar over your hips.

There are a number of errors to avoid with the power jerk. These are going to be discussed by the phase of the exercise that they occur in.

- *The start:* The two major errors seen at the start involve the back set and the grip. Failing to keep the back set and the chest inflated will cause your shoulders to slump forward. This will cause the weight to shift forward, making it more difficult to control. Another error seen in the start is to grip the bar too wide. This is frequently caused by using the same grip on the bar that you would on the bench press. This makes it more difficult to control the bar.

- *The dip:* There are two major errors with the dip. One is associated with speed and the other is associated with squat technique. Beginners will frequently perform the dip slowly. This is a problem because it diminishes how much elastic energy can be generated from the combination of the dip and the drive and this will make the exercise more difficult. The other error occurs when the squat is performed by bending the knees first. If the squat is performed from the knees, instead of the hips, smaller muscles are primarily being used in the exercise, which means less force can be generated.

- *The drive:* The major error seen with the drive is to perform it slowly. Pausing in the bottom of the squat, or driving up slowly, will cause the elastic energy to dissipate, making the exercise much more difficult.

- *The squat under:* With the squat under, the two major problems deal with foot placement and bar placement. Spreading the feet too far apart will create balance problems. Likewise, placing the bar too far forward or too far backwards (i.e. not over the hips) will make control over the bar very difficult.

Power Jerk Variations

The power jerk has several variations that may be performed. These exercises are explosive in nature and may be used for variety. This chapter will cover a number of variations that are possible with the power jerk. These variations include:

- push jerk;
- behind the neck push press, jerk grip; and
- behind the neck push press, snatch grip.

The push jerk is more of a strengthening exercise for the upper body than the power jerk is. However, it is still explosive in nature. With this exercise, begin with the bar on the front of your shoulders. Just like with the power jerk, dip and drive the weight off your shoulders. Unlike the power jerk, there is no squat under. When the bar has been driven to its maximum height (i.e. eye level), press the bar up and slightly behind your head. Remember to get the bar in line with your hips.

The behind the neck push press with a jerk grip begins with the barbell on the back of your shoulders. Perform this exercise standing up with your feet hip-width apart. Grip the bar with a jerk-width, pronated grip. Take a deep breath, hold it, and set your back. Make sure your elbows are directly under the bar. From the start, dip and drive the weight off your shoulders. When the weight slows its ascent, complete the exercise by pressing the weight up. Remember to keep the bar over your hips and make sure you do not slam the bar into the back of your head.

The behind the neck push press with a snatch grip begins with the barbell on the back of your shoulders. Perform this exercise standing up with your feet hip-width apart. Grip the bar with a snatch-width, pronated grip (see later in this chapter for more about the snatch grip). Take a deep breath, hold it, and set your back. Make sure your elbows are directly under the bar. From the start, dip and drive the weight off your shoulders. When the weight slows its ascent, complete the exercise by pressing the weight up.

THE POWER SNATCH

The power snatch is another total body exercise that develops explosiveness. It also develops balance and proprioception. It is used extensively in the training of weightlifters and athletes. Like the power clean and power jerk, this exercise involves high speeds, exerting force against the ground, and is performed standing up. It too is thought to have a great deal of transfer over to the playing field. This chapter will discuss how to perform the power snatch, what common errors to avoid, and how to perform and use variations of this exercise.

The power snatch is divided into several phases:

1. the start, where you interact with the barbell while it is on the platform;
2. the first pull, where you lift the barbell to knee height;
3. the second pull, where the barbell achieves its maximum velocity;
4. the nonsupport phase, where you are not in contact with the ground as your lift the barbell to its maximum height;
5. the amortization phase, where you drop under the barbell and "catch" it overhead on fully extended arms; and
6. the finish, where you stand up with the barbell overhead on fully extended arms.

Before discussing how to perform the power snatch we should discuss how to select your grip-width on this exercise. Because this exercise requires you to squat with a weight held over your head, it requires a wider grip-width than the power clean or power jerk. To determine your grip-width, you will need another person's assistance.

Have someone stand behind you with a tape measure. Keeping your left arm at your side, raise your right arm until it is parallel to the floor. Make a fist with your right hand. Measure from your left shoulder to the end of your right fist. Mark that distance on the barbell. You should grip the bar just outside those marks.

Power Snatch Technique

Begin the power snatch with the barbell on the platform. Approach the bar and stand in front of it so that your feet are approximately hip-width apart. Take a snatch-width, pronated grip on the barbell. Once you have gripped the bar, squat down and attempt to put your stomach between your legs. As you do this take a deep breath, hold it, and set your back. Pull the bar against your shins. Your shoulders should be in front of the barbell with your arms straight and your elbows rotated out.

If this is done properly, then your shoulders will be ahead of the bar and your hips will be slightly higher than your knees. Your chest and abdomen should be protruding.

Perform the first pull in a slow, controlled manner. Just like with the clean, ripping the barbell off the floor may result in many errors that can add up and result in a missed lift. To perform the first pull, extend your knees and hips to lift the barbell. Your hips and shoulders should travel up at the same speed. During the first pull, as your knees extend, the barbell should move back towards your body a few centimeters.

If the first pull is done properly, then your shoulders will remain in front of the bar. Your arms should remain straight and your back should remain set.

When the bar reaches the height of the knees, continue extending your knees and hips until the barbell scrapes your hips. Once the bar reaches the height of your hips, extend your hips and violently shrug the bar up as you rise up onto your toes. During the second pull, your shoulders will move from being in front of the barbell to being behind it. If the second pull is done properly then the force imparted to the bar will force it to move up the body.

Follow through with the second pull by moving your feet from hip-width to shoulder-width. The bar should continue moving up during this phase.

When the bar reaches its maximum height during the nonsupport phase (approximately chest-height), you should pull yourself under the bar. This should be done so that you catch the bar in a $1/4$ squat. When your feet hit the ground your arms should be locked out overhead. You should catch the bar with your hips pushed back and your knees bent. The bar should be caught so that it is in line with your hips. This is important for balance. If the barbell is not in line with your hips, you will be off balance which will make the exercise more difficult.

From the $1/4$ squat, stand up with the bar overhead. Keep your arms locked out.

There are a number of common errors to avoid with the power snatch. These are going to be discussed by the phase of the lift that they occur in:

■ *The start:* The most common error involves not having the back set during the start.

■ *The first pull:* As with the start, one of the common errors involves pulling with a rounded back. Another is to let your hips travel up faster than your shoulders.

■ *The second pull:* As with the clean, common errors include performing the second pull in parts and performing it by thrusting the hips forward.

■ *The nonsupport/amortization phase:* Catching the barbell on the toes (i.e. feet are not flat) will cause the lifter to lose the barbell in front of them. Catching the barbell on bent arms will also typically result in the lifter losing the barbell in front of them. Another common error performed here has to do with how the squat is executed. If the squat is executed by pushing the knees forward (as opposed to sitting back into the squat), then this will make balance very difficult.

Power Snatch Variations

The power snatch has several variations that may be performed. These variations include:

■ overhead squats;

■ power snatches from the hang;

■ power snatches from blocks; and

■ snatch pulls.

Overhead squats teach you to balance when squatting with a weight overhead. It is also a great conditioning exercise for the muscles of the lower extremity, core, and shoulder. To perform the overhead squat, start out with the bar on the back of your shoulders. Grip the bar with a pronated, snatch-width grip. Take a deep breath, hold it, and set your back. Move your feet so that they are shoulder-width apart. Keeping your elbows under the bar, press the bar so that it is overhead. Keep the bar in line with your hips. With your arms straight, push your hips back and squat down with the weight overhead.

There are a number of things to remember when performing this exercise. You must keep your feet flat on the ground while performing the squat. Otherwise, the weight will be shifted forward making balance impossible. Perform the squat by pushing your hips back and then bending your knees. Just pushing your knees forward will shift the bar forward. During the entire squat (up and down) you should push against the bar with your arms. This will help you keep your arms straight. Bending your arms will make the exercise more difficult and will make balance impossible.

The power snatch from the hang teaches technique by emphasizing portions of the lift. It develops back strength by requiring you to hold the bar in the starting positions. It also emphasizes the second pull, so it may be used to enhance explosiveness. In fact, according to Bartonietz (1996), joint power reaches higher levels when the lift is performed from the hang than when it is performed competitively.

There are three primary variations possible with the power snatch from the hang. It may be performed with the barbell starting out above the knees. It may be performed with the barbell starting out at knee height. It may also be performed with the barbell starting out at below the knee height.

To perform the power snatch from the hang, with the barbell above the knees, begin by taking a snatch-width grip on the barbell and standing up with it in your hands. Your feet should be hip-width apart. Set your back. From this position, push your hips back and unlock your knees. Do this until the bar reaches your hip or thighs. From that position, keeping your arms straight, perform a slight dip with your knees and then execute the power snatch.

To perform the power snatch from the hang, with the barbell at knee height, begin by standing up with the barbell in your hands. As previously described, lower the bar until it reaches your thighs. At this point, continue pushing your hips back and bend your knees until you lower the bar to knee height. From this point perform the power snatch.

To perform the power snatch from the hang, with the barbell at below the knee height, begin by standing up with the barbell in your hands. As previously described, lower the bar until it reaches knee height. Continue lowering the bar until it is below your knees. From this point perform the power snatch.

Like power snatches from the hang, power snatches from blocks may also be performed from above the knee height, from knee height, and from below knee height.

With these variations, the bar beings on blocks. This means one does not need to posses the same amount of back strength to perform them. With the exception of the barbell beginning on blocks, the exercise is performed just like it is from the hang.

Snatch pulls may be performed from the hang or from blocks. They may be performed from the floor, from above the knees, from the knees, and from below the knees. They are performed like clean pulls, except a snatch-width grip is used instead.

REFERENCES

1. Aagaard, P. (2003). Training-induced changes in neural function. *Exercise and Sport Sciences Reviews,* 31(2), 61-67.

2. Anderson, E.A. (1997). *EMG and strength in trunk and hip muscles – particularly the iliopsoas* (Thesis). Stockholm: Karolinska Institute.

3. Ariel, B.G. (1974). Biomechanical analysis of the knee joint during deep knee bends with heavy load. In Nelson, R.C. and Morehouse, C.A. (Eds.). *Biomechanics IV, International Series on Sports Science, 1,* University Park Press, Baltimore, Md, 45-52.

4. Armitage-Johnson, S. (1994a). A safe training environment, part III, maintaining equipment. *Strength and Conditioning,* 16(3), 54-55.

5. Armitage-Johnson, S. (1989). Maintaining a safe environment in the strength facility. *NSCA Journal,* 11(6), 56-57.

6. Armitage-Johnson, S. (1990). Maintaining strength facility areas. *NSCA Journal,* 12(1), 24-25.

7. Armitage-Johnson, S. (1994b). Providing a safe training environment for participants, part I. *Strength and Conditioning,* 16(1), 64-65.

8. Axler, C.T. & S.M. McGill. (1997). Low back loads over a variety of abdominal exercises: Searching for the safest abdominal challenge. *Medicine and Science in Sports and Exercise,* 29, 804-810.

9. Baechle, T. & R. Earle. (Eds). (2000). *Essentials of Strength Training and Conditioning,* 2nd Edition. Champaign, Il: Human Kinetics.

10. Baratta, R., M. Solomonow, B.H. Zhou, D. Letson, R. Chuinard, & R. D'Ambrosia. (1988). Muscular coactivation: The role of the antagonist musculature in maintaining knee stability. *The American Journal of Sports Medicine,* 16(2),113-122.

11. Bartonietz, K.E. (1996). Biomechanics of the snatch: Toward a higher training efficiency. *Strength and Conditioning,* 18(3), 24-31.

12. Behm, D.G. & D.G. Sale. (1993). Velocity specificity of resistance training. *Sports Medicine,* 15(6), 374-388.

13. Beim, G.M., J.L. Giraldo, D.M. Pincivero, M.J. Borror, & F.H. Fu. (1997). Abdominal strengthening exercises: A comparative EMG study. *Journal of Sport Rehabilitation,* 6, 11-20.

14. Bloomer, R.J. & J.C. Ives. (2000). Varying neural and hypertrophic influences in a strength program. *Strength and Conditioning Journal,* 22(2), 30-35.

15. Bompa, T.O. (1999). *Periodization: Theory and Methodology of Training* 4th Edition. Champaign, Il: Human Kinetics.

16. Bompa, T. (1994). *Power Training for Sport.* New York: Mosaic Press.

17. Bondarchuk, A. (1988a). Constructing a training system, part I. *Track Technique,* 102, 3254-3259.

18. Bondarchuk, A. (1988b). Constructing a training system, part II. *Track Technique,* 103, 3286-3288.

19. Bowerman, W.J. & W.H. Freeman. (1991). *High-Performance Training for Track and Field* 2nd Edition. Champaign, Il: Leisure Press.

20. Brawdy, P. (1987). Manipulating the variables of intensity through exercise selection and intensity. *NSCA Journal,* 9(3), 60-61.

21. Brewer, V., B.M. Meyer, M.S. Keele, S.J. Upton, & R.D. Hagan. (1983). Role of exercise in prevention of involutional bone loss. *Medicine and Science in Sports and Exercise,* 15(6), 445-449

22. Brooks, G.A., T.D. Fahey, & T.P. White. (1996). *Exercise Physiology: Human Bioenergetics And Its Applications* 2nd Edition. Mountain View, CA: Mayfield Publishing Company.

23. Burgener, M. (1994). Jumping drills as warm-up. *Strength and Conditioning, 16*(1), 44-45.

24. Calbet, J.A.L., P. Diaz Herrera, & L.P. Rodriguez. (1999). High bone mineral density in male elite professional volleyball players. *Osteoporosis International, 10*, 468-474.

25. Chandler, T.J. & M.H. Stone. (1992). The squat exercise in athletic conditioning: A review of the literature. NSCA.

26. Chandler, T.J., G.D Wilson, & M.H. Stone. (1989). The effect of the squat exercise on knee stability. *Medicine and Science in Sports and Exercise, 21*(3), 299-303.

27. Chang, D.E., Burschbacher, L.P., and Edlich, R.F. (1988). Limited joint mobility in power lifters. *The American Journal of Sports Medicine, 16*(3), 280-284.

28. Charniga, Jr., A. (1986). Variations and rational use of the good morning exercise. *NSCA Journal, 8*(1), 74-77.

29. Charniga, Jr., A., V. Gambetta, W. Kraemer, H. Newton, H.S. O'Bryant, G. Palmieri, J. Pedemonte, D. Pfaff, & M.H. Stone. (1986). Periodization, part 1. *NSCA Journal, 8*(5), 12-22.

30. Chu, D.A. (1998). *Jumping Into Plyometrics* 2nd Edition. Champaign, Il: Leisure Press.

31. Ciocca, Jr., M. (2000). Pneumothorax in a weight lifter. *The Physician and Sportsmedicine, 28*(4), 97-103.

32. Cissik, J.M. (1998). *An Introduction to Olympic-Style Weightlifting* 2nd Edition. New York: The McGraw-Hill Companies Inc.

33. Cissik, J.M. (2002). Basic principles of strength training and conditioning. *Performance Training Journal, 1*(4), 7-11.

34. Cissik, J.M. (2000). Coaching the front squat. *Strength and Conditioning Journal, 22*(5), 7-12.

35. Cissik, J.M. (2000). Conditioning for hammer throwers. *Track & Field Coaches Review, 73*(1), 32-34.

36. Cissik, J.M. (2005). Is periodization dead or just very sick? *Track Coach, 170*, 5422-5427.

37. Cissik, J.M. (2004). Means and methods of speed training, part I. *Strength and Conditioning Journal, 26*(4), 24-29.

38. Cissik, J.M. (2004). Plyometric fundamentals. *Performance Training Journal, 3*(2), 9-13.

39. Cissik, J.M. (2002). Programming abdominal training, part I. *Strength and Conditioning Journal, 24*(1), 9-15.

40. Cissik, J.M. (2002). Programming abdominal training, part 2. *Strength and Conditioning Journal, 24*(2), 9-12.

41. Cissik, J.M. (2003). *Strength Training for Track and Field.* Mountain View, CA: TAFNEWS Press.

42. Cissik, J.M. (2002). Technique and speed development for running. *Performance Training Journal, 1*(8), 18-22.

43. Cissik, J.M. & M. Barnes. (2004). *Sport Speed and Agility.* Monterey, CA: Coaches Choice.

44. Clark, K.M., et al. (2003). EMG comparison of the upper and lower rectus abdominus during abdominal exercises. *Journal of Strength and Conditioning Research, 17*(3), 475-483.

45. Conroy, B.P., W.J. Kraemer, C.M. Maresh, S.J. Fleck, M.H. Stone, A.C. Fry, P.D. Miller, & G.P. Dalsky. (1993). Bone mineral density in elite junior Olympic weightlifters. *Medicine and Science in Sports and Exercise, 25*(10), 1103-1109.

46. Cooper, D., J. Vellutini, O. Whaley, J. Duval, R. Bojak, B. Harbach, M. Breitenbach, E. Troxel, & J. Earles. (1991). High school weightroom safety: part I. *NSCA Journal, 13*(3), 10-18.

47. Cosio-Lima, L.M., et al. (2003). Effects of physioball and conventional floor exercises on early phase adaptations in back and abdominal core stability and balance in women. *Journal of Strength and Conditioning Research, 17*(4), 721-725.

48. Dahlkvist, N.J., Mayo, P., and Seedhom, B.B. (1982). Forces during squatting and rising from a deep squat. *Engineering in Medicine, 11*(2), 69-76.

49. Draganich, L.F., Jaeger, R.J., and Kralj, A.R. (1989). Coactivation of the hamstrings and quadriceps during extension of the knee. *Journal of Bone and Joint Surgery, 71A*(7), 1075-1081.

50. Dunn, B., K. Klein, B. Kroll, T.M. McLaughlin, P. O'Shea, & D. Wathen. (1984). The squat and its application to athletic performance. *NSCA Journal, 6*(3), 10-22, 68.

51. Elam, R. (1986). Warm-up and athletic performance: A physiological analysis. *NSCA Journal, 8*(2), 30-33.

52. Escamilla, R.F. (2001). Knee biomechanics of the dynamic squat exercise. *Medicine and Science in Sports & Exercise* 33(1), 127-141.

53. Escamilla, R.F., A.C. Francisco, G.S. Fleisig, S.W. Barrentine, C.M. Welch, A.V. Kayes, K.P. Speer, & J.R. Andrews. (2000). A three-dimensional biomechanical analysis of sumo and conventional deadlifts. *Medicine and Science in Sports and Exercise,* 32(7), 1265-1275.

54. Escamilla, R.F., et al. (2002). An EMG analysis of sumo and conventional deadlifts. *Medicine and Science in Sports & Exercise,* 34(4), 682-688.

55. Escamilla, R.F., et al. (2001). A three-dimensional biomechanical analysis of the squat during varying stance widths. *Medicine and Science in Sports & Exercise,* 33(6), 984-998.

56. Escamilla, R.F., et al. (2000). A three-dimensional biomechanical analysis of sumo and conventional style deadlifts. *Medicine and Science in Sports & Exercise,* 32(7), 1265-1275.

57. Escamilla, R.F., et al. (2001). Effects of technique variations on knee biomechanics during the squat and leg press. *Medicine and Science in Sports & Exercise,* 33(9), 1552-1566.

58. Farley, K. (1995). Analysis of the conventional deadlift. *Strength and Conditioning,* 17(6), 55-57.

59. Flint, M.M. (1965). Abdominal muscle involvement during the performance of various forms of sit-up exercise. *American Journal of Physical Medicine,* 44(5), 224-234.

60. Fluck, M., et al. (2000). Skeletal muscle calcium-independent kinase activity increases during either hypertrophy or running. Journal of Applied Physiology, 88, 352-358.

61. Freeman, J. (1989). Guidelines for safe and effective strength program administration. *NSCA Journal,* 11(2), 26-28.

62. Freeman, W. (1994). Coaching, periodization, and the battle of artist versus scientist. *Track Technique,* 127, 4054-4057.

63. Fry, A. (1986). Proper attire. *NSCA Journal,* 8(6), 42.

64. Fry, A. (1985). Weight room safety. *NSCA Journal,* 7(4), 32-33.

65. Gambetta, V. (1991a). Concept and application of periodization. *NSCA Journal,* 13(5), 64-66.

66. Gambetta, V. (1991b). Some thoughts on new trends in training theory. *NSCA Journal,* 13(1), 24-26.

67. Garhammer, J. (1993). A review of power output studies of Olympic and powerlifting: Methodology, performance, prediction, and evaluation tests. *Journal of Strength and Conditioning Research,* 7(2), 76-89.

68. Guyton, A.C. (1991). *Textbook of Medical Physiology.* 8th Edition. Philadelphia: W.B. Saunders Company, 67-88, 98.

69. Halling, D. (1991). Safety considerations - spotting. *NSCA Journal,* 13(2), 54-55.

70. Harre, D. (Ed.). (1982). *Principles of Sports Training: Introduction to the Theory and Methods of Training.* Berlin: Sportverlag.

71. Hedrick, A. (1993). Literature review: High-speed resistance training. *NSCA Journal,* 15(6), 22-30.

72. Hedrick, A. (1995). Training for hypertrophy. *Strength and Conditioning,* 17(3), 22-29.

73. Hedrick, A. (2000). Training the trunk for improved athletic performance. *Strength and Conditioning Journal,* 22(3), 50-61.

74. Hunter, G.R. (1994). Muscle physiology. In Baechle, T.R. (Ed.). *Essentials of Strength Training and Conditioning.* Champaign, IL: Human Kinetics, Il, 3-9.

75. Javorek, I. (1993). Specificity in sports conditioning. *NSCA Journal,* 15(6), 31-33.

76. Jones, C.S., C. Christensen, & M. Young. (2000). Weight training injury trends: A 20-year survey. *The Physician and Sportsmedicine,* 28(7), 61-72.

77. Kahehisa, H. & M. Miyashito. (1983). Specificity of velocity in strength training. *European Journal of Applied Physiology,* 52, 104-106.

78. Kawakami, Y., et al. (1995). Training-induced changes in muscle architecture and specific tension. *European Journal of Applied Physiology,* 72, 37-43.

79. Kawakami, Y., et al. (2000). Architecture of contracting human muscles and its functional significance. *Journal of Applied Biomechanics,* 16, 88-98.

80. Kernan, J. (1999). The 24 consensus principles of athletic training and conditioning. *Track Coach,* 148, 4720-4722.

81. Kirksey, B. & M.H. Stone. (1998). Periodizing a college sprint program: Theory and practice. *Strength and Conditioning,* 20(3), 42-47.

82. Klein, K.K. (1961). The deep squat exercise as utilized in weight training for athletics and its effect on the ligaments of the knee. *Journal of the Association of Physical and Mental Rehabilitation*, 15(1), 6-11, 23.

83. Kraemer, W.J. (1984b). Exercise prescription-order of exercises. *NSCA Journal*, 6(4), 47.

84. Kraemer, W.J., S.J. Fleck, & M. Deschenes. (1988). A review: Factors in exercise prescription of resistance training. *NSCA Journal*, 10(5), 36-41.

85. Krolner, B., B. Toft, S.P. Nielsen, & E. Tondevold. (1983). Physical exercise as prophylaxis against involuntary vertebral bone loss: A controlled trial. *Clinical Exercise*, 64, 541-546.

86. Kumagai, K., et al. (2000). Sprint performance is related to muscle fascicle length in male 100-meter sprinters. *Journal of Applied Physiology*, 88, 811-816.

87. Kurz, T. (1991). *Science of Sports Training: How to Plan and Control Training for Peak Performance*. Island Pond, VT: Stadion Publishing Company.

88. LaFontaine, T. (1999). Resistance training and bone health. *Strength and Conditioning Journal*, 21(1), 11-12.

89. McArdle, W.D., F.I., Katch, & V.L. Katch. (1996). *Exercise Physiology: Energy, Nutrition, and Human Performance*. 4th Edition. Philadelphia: Lea & Febiger.

90. McBride, J.M., T. Triplett-McBride, A. Davie, & R.U. Newton. (1999). A comparison of strength and power characteristics between power lifters, Olympic lifters, and sprinters. *Journal of Strength and Conditioning Research*, 13(1), 58-66.

91. McCall, G.E., et al. (1996). Muscle fiber hypertrophy, hyperplasia, and capillary density in college men after resistance training. *Journal of Applied Physiology*, 81, 2004-2012.

92. McFarlane, B. (1987). Warm-up design patterns. *NSCA Journal*, 9(4), 22-30.

93. McGill, S.M. (1995). The mechanics of torso flexion: sit ups and standing dynamic flexion manoeuvres. *Clinical Biomechanics*, 10(4), 184-192.

94. Matveyev, L. (1981). *Fundamentals of Sports Training*. Moscow: Progress Publishers.

95. Medvedyev, A.S. (1986). *A System of Multi-Year Training in Weightlifting*. Translated by Charniga, Jr., A. Livonia, Michigan: Sportivny Press.

96. Meyers, E.J. (1971). Effect of selected exercise variables on ligament stability and flexibility of the knee. *The Research Quarterly*, 42(4), 411-422.

97. Nguyen, T.V., P.N. Sambrook, & J.A. Eisman. (1998). Bone loss, physical activity, and weight change in elderly women: The Dubbo osteoporosis epidemiology study. *Journal of Bone and Mineral Research*, 13(9), 1458-1467.

98. Nutter, J. (1986). Physical activity increases bone density. *NSCA Journal*, 8(3), 67-69.

99. O'Shea, P. (1999). Towards an understanding of power. *Strength and Conditioning Journal*, 21(5), 34-35.

100. Palmitier, R.A., Kai-Nan, A., Scott, S.G., and Chao, E.Y.S. (1991). Kinetic chain exercise in knee rehabilitation. *Sports Medicine*, 11(6), 402-413.

101. Plisk, S.S. & M.H. Stone. (2003). Periodization strategies. *Strength and Conditioning Journal*, 25(6), 19-37.

102. Rhodes, E.C., A.D. Martin, J.E. Taunton, M. Donnelly, J. Warren, & J. Elliot. (2000). Effects of one year of resistance training on the relation between muscular strength and bone density in elderly women. *British Journal of Sports Medicine*, 34, 18-22.

103. Risser, W. L. (1990). Musculoskeletal injuries caused by weight training. *Clinical Pediatrics*, 29(6), 305-310.

104. Sabo, D., L. Bernd, J. Pfeil, & A. Reiter. (1996). Bone quality in the lumbar spine in high-performance athletes. *European Spine Journal*, 5, 258-263.

105. Sanborn, C.F. (1990). Exercise, calcium, and bone density. *Gatorade Sports Science Institute Sports Science Exchange*, 2(24).

106. Shellock, F. (1986). Physiological, psychological and injury prevention aspects of warm-up. *NSCA Journal*, 8(5), 24-27.

107. Signorile, J.F., A.J. Zink, & S.P. Szwed. (2002). A comparative EMG investigation of muscle activity patterns using various hand positions during the lat pulldown. *Journal of Strength and Conditioning Research*, 16(4), 539-546.

108. Silvey, S. (1994). *World Class All Sports Speed Training Program* 2nd Edition.

109. Staron, R.S. (1997). Human skeletal muscle fiber types: Delineation, development, and distribution. *Canadian Journal of Applied Physiology*, 22(4), 307-327.

110. Stone, M.H., H. O'Bryant, & J. Garhammer. (1981). Hypothetical model for strength training. *Journal of Sports Medicine and Physical Fitness,* 21(4), 342-351.

111. Stone, M.H. (1994). *Position Paper and Literature Review: Explosive Exercises and Training.* National Strength and Conditioning Association, Colorado Springs, CO.

112. Stone, M.H., D. Collins, S. Plisk, G. Haff, & M.E. Stone. (2000). Training principles: Evaluation of modes and methods of resistance training. *Strength and Conditioning Journal,* 22(3), 65-76.

113. Stone, M.H. & R.A. Borden. (1997). Modes and methods of resistance training. *Strength and Conditioning,* 19(4), 18-25.

114. Thompson, P.J.L. (1991). *Introduction to Coaching Theory.* Monaco: International Amateur Athletic Federation.

115. Thomson, R., B. Fix, P. White, R. Moran, P. Longo, D. Van Halanger, & B. Rohde. (1989). Weightroom supervision and maintenance. *NSCA Journal,* 11(3), 14-22.

116. Todd, T. (1984). Karl Klein and the squat. *NSCA Journal,* 6(3), 26-31, 67.

117. Verkoshansky, Y. (1999). The end of "periodisation" of training in top-class sport. *New Studies in Athletics,* 14(1), 47-55.

118. Wagner, D.R. (1996). Skeletal muscle growth: Hypertrophy and hyperplasia. *Strength and Conditioning,* 18(5), 38-39.

119. Walters, C.E. & M.J. Partridge. (1957). Electromyographic study of the differential action of the abdominal muscles during exercise. *American Journal of Physical Medicine,* 36(5), 259-268.

120. Wathen, D. (1987). Flexibility – its place in warm up activities. *NSCA Journal,* 9(5), 26-27.

121. Wilmore, J.H. & D.L. Costill. (1994). *Physiology of Sport and Exercise.* Champaign, IL: Human Kinetics.

122. Woo, S.L.Y., S.C. Kuei, D. Amiel, M.A. Gomez, W.C. Hayes, F.C. White, & W.H. Akeson. (1981). The effect of prolonged physical training on the properties of long bone: A study of Wolff's Law. *The Journal of Bone and Joint Surgery,* 63-A(5), 780-786.

123. Wretenberg, P., Y. Feng, & U.P. Arborelius. (1996). High- and low-bar squatting techniques during weight training. *Medicine and Science in Sports and Exercise,* 28(2), 218-224.

124. Wright, G.A., et al. (1999). Electromyographic activity of the hamstrings during performance of the leg curl, stiff-leg deadlift, and back squat movements. *Journal of Strength and Conditioning Research,* 13(2), 168-174.

125. Yan, Z. (2000). Skeletal muscle adaptation and cell cycle regulation. *Exercise and Sport Sciences Reviews,* 28(1), 24-26.

126. Young, W. (1991). The planning of resistance training for power sports. *NSCA Journal,* 13(4), 26-29.

127. Zatsiorsky, V.M. (1995). *The Science and Practice of Strength Training.* Champaign, IL: Human Kinetics.

128. Zemper, E. D. (1990). Four-year study of weightroom injuries in a national sample of college football teams. *NSCA Journal,* 12(3), 32-34.

ABOUT THE AUTHOR

John Cissik is the Director of Fitness and Recreation at Texas Woman's University where he is also an adjunct professor. He serves as the strength and conditioning consultant for the University of North Texas's track and field team and runs his own business, Fitness and Conditioning Enterprises, which provides speed and agility instruction to young athletes.

He holds bachelor's and master's degrees in Kinesiology. He is a Certified Strength and Conditioning Specialist from the National Strength and Conditioning Association. In addition, he holds personal training certifications from the American Council on Exercise and the National Strength and Conditioning Association. He is also a level 2 coach in sprints from USA Track and Field, where he is also a graduate of their Instructor Training Course and has been a certified club coach from USA Weightlifting.

John has written three other books on strength and speed training and over 60 lay and coaching articles. He has been in publications such as *IRONMAN, Muscle and Fitness, Muscular Development, Performance Training Journal, Pure Power, Strength and Conditioning Journal, Track Coach, and Track and Field Coaches Review*. In addition to books and articles, he's also been in three videos on strength training.

He has served as the Texas State Director for the National Strength and Conditioning Association and has put on and spoken at a variety of strength and conditioning clinics and conferences. In addition he has spoken for other professional organizations such as the National Intramural-Recreational Sports Association and the Texas Association for Health, Physical Education, Recreation, and Dance. He has also provided continuing education for the American Council on Exercise and the Aerobics and Fitness Association of America.

In addition to his professional activities John enjoys working out, reading history and philosophy, playing chess, and spending time with his wife, son, dogs, and cats.